SARA BARKER

CHANGE-THE-SETTING

4
PREFACE
FIONA BRADLEY / JONATHAN WATKINS

54
PRESENTNESS IS GRACE
KATHARINE STOUT

132
MAKING IT EVEN NEWER
ALI SMITH

150 LIST OF ILLUSTRATIONS
154 BIOGRAPHY
156 ACKNOWLEDGEMENTS

PREFACE

FIONA BRADLEY / JONATHAN WATKINS

> The creation of worlds, nothing could be simpler
> Magdalena Tulli, *Moving Parts*, 2015

The worlds Sara Barker makes occupy the boundary between sculpture, painting and drawing. Working with rods of steel and aluminium, sheets of glass, and painted sections, she defines and delineates, playing plane against line and volume against emptiness to draw a viewer into her visual imagination. Sometimes wall based, sometimes floor based, and sometimes moving from floor to wall and back again, Barker's work inhabits space and also describes it. She is interested in how space may exist in the mind – in novels, in memory – and there is a quiet eloquence to the things she makes that seems to hint at this kind of spatial imagining.

This book presents art Barker has made since 2008. It follows the journey her work has been on, charting new developments, taking note of repeating consistencies. The two exhibitions the book accompanies – one at The Fruitmarket Gallery, Edinburgh and one at Ikon Gallery, Birmingham – present both the consistencies and the developments with two major sequences of new work brought into conversation with selected existing works. The newest works, some of which are illustrated in this publication, pick up, expand upon, refute, complicate and develop the questions

Barker's work has been posing since its earliest beginnings. *CHANGE-THE-SETTING*, the title of the book, is part of one of the new works' titles, and is intended to function like a stage direction, an exhortation to change one element in order to allow the others to recombine into a new imagined world.

Language – both written and sculptural – is generative as well as descriptive. When a writer describes a place, whether imagined or remembered, that space opens up in the mind of the reader. This happens every time the words are encountered, the space changing to meet the changing circumstances of each reader and even each read. So also with art: Barker's structures outline, contain, inhabit and ultimately create not only one space but several shifting spaces, their constituent parts moving over each other as you walk towards, away and around them. They seek connections both imagined and real, reminding us of picture or window frames, of figures, of furniture, of places we have known or would like to have known.

This book, designed in close collaboration with the artist, moves more or less chronologically through her practice, though it begins as well as ends with work made just before it went to press. It highlights the importance within her practice of writing and reading as well as looking and making, pulling the titles of the works away from the images of them, encouraging us to pay new attention to the titles as one of the layers the artist uses to describe and create her sequences of worlds. The book includes a new essay by curator and writer Katharine Stout, and a new piece of writing by the author Ali Smith. Stout has been following Barker's work for some years, and her text encompasses the breadth of Barker's practice, looking at the techniques, processes and affects developed as the work progresses. Stout draws on her broad understanding of drawing and painting practice to highlight the importance of drawing, painting and reading as part of the making of the work, looking at how Barker works between the sculptural and the pictorial, conflating image and object. Ali Smith's engagement with the work is more recent – she visited Barker's studio while she was making the new work for the exhibitions, and has written a text in response to it. Called 'Making it even newer', the text is a coming together of the written and the visual, a dialogue between two artistic sensibilities, Smith's elastic and inventive language more than a match for Barker's work, which she characterises as something which is 'all movement between form and form, painting and sculpture, figurative and abstract, metal and air, oil and water, and everything in dialogue, like a natural weighing-up of things is happening in each piece, and even between the pieces as the eye happens on them'.

We are very grateful to Katharine Stout and Ali Smith for contributing such insightful pieces of writing to this publication. We thank Sara Barker's galleries, Mary Mary in Glasgow, carlier | gebauer in Berlin, and The Approach in London, for their support of the artist and of this publication, and we thank Creative Scotland for the considerable financial contribution they have made to the development of new work for the exhibitions.

Above all, though, we thank Sara Barker. For her commitment to the project and her hard work in seeing it through, and for sharing with us the spatial intricacies of her imagination.

Fiona Bradley, Director, The Fruitmarket Gallery, Edinburgh
Jonathan Watkins, Director, Ikon Gallery, Birmingham

geographies of Dust and Air
moving parts out of night
brass and stainless steel rod,
folded aluminium sheet, glass,
perspex, automotive paint,
spray paint

Minerva made a dream to order
Patterns she saw as signs
stainless steel and brass rod,
folded aluminium sheet, glass,
perspex, automotive paint,
spray paint

What's the medium?
A medium for their mediums
CHANGE-THE-SETTING
stainless steel rod, folded
aluminium sheet, glass, perspex,
automotive paint, spray paint

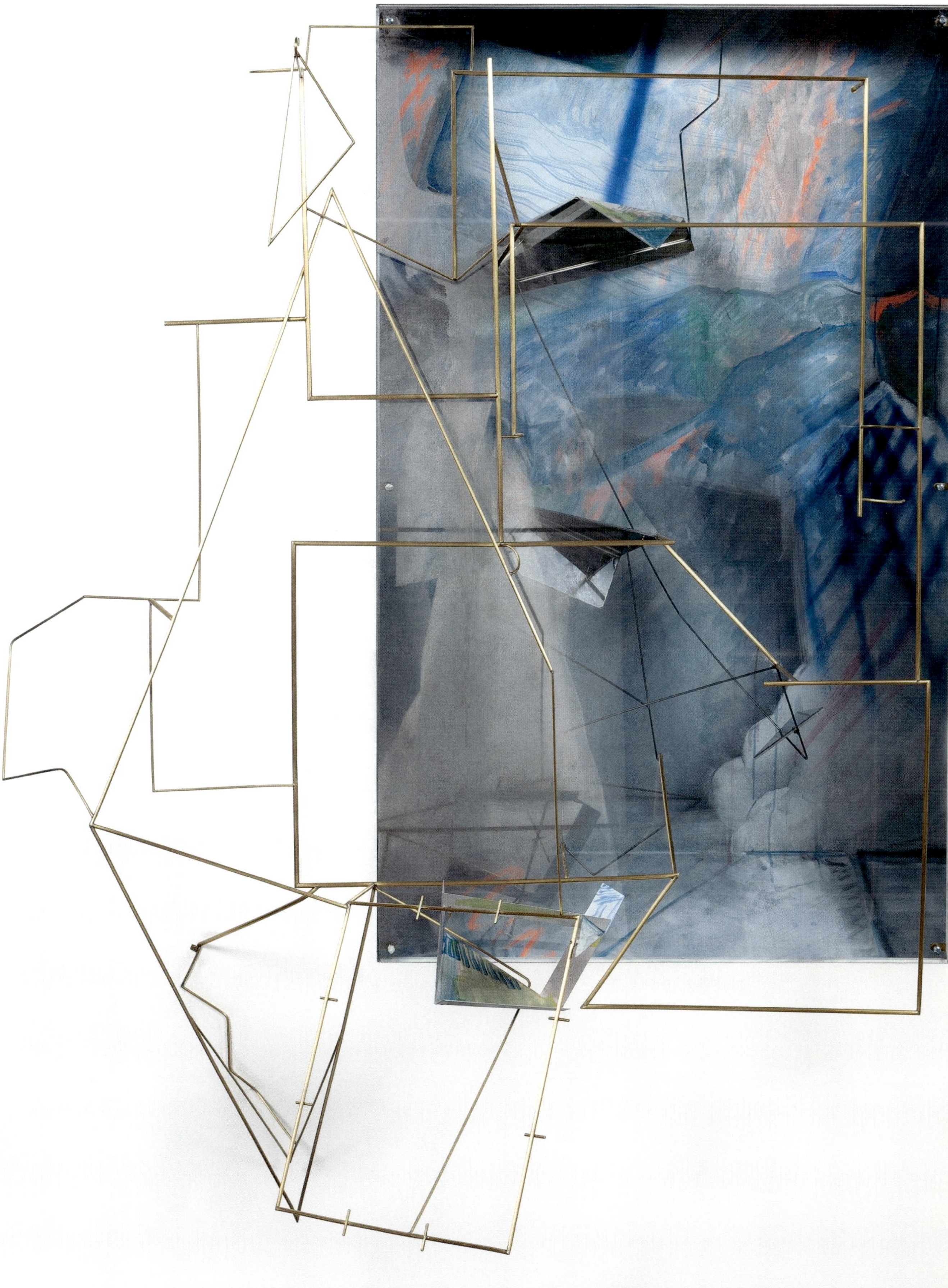

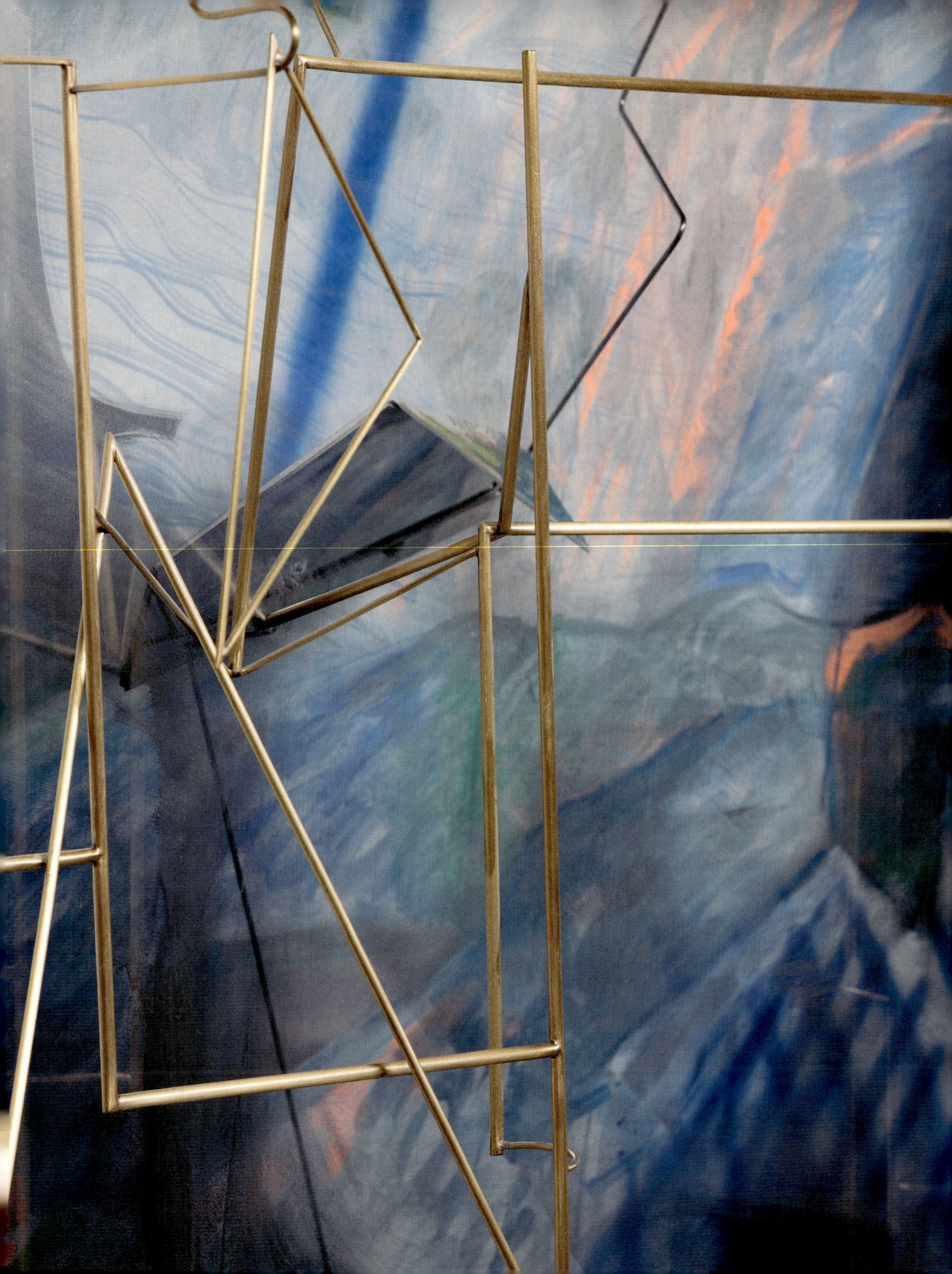

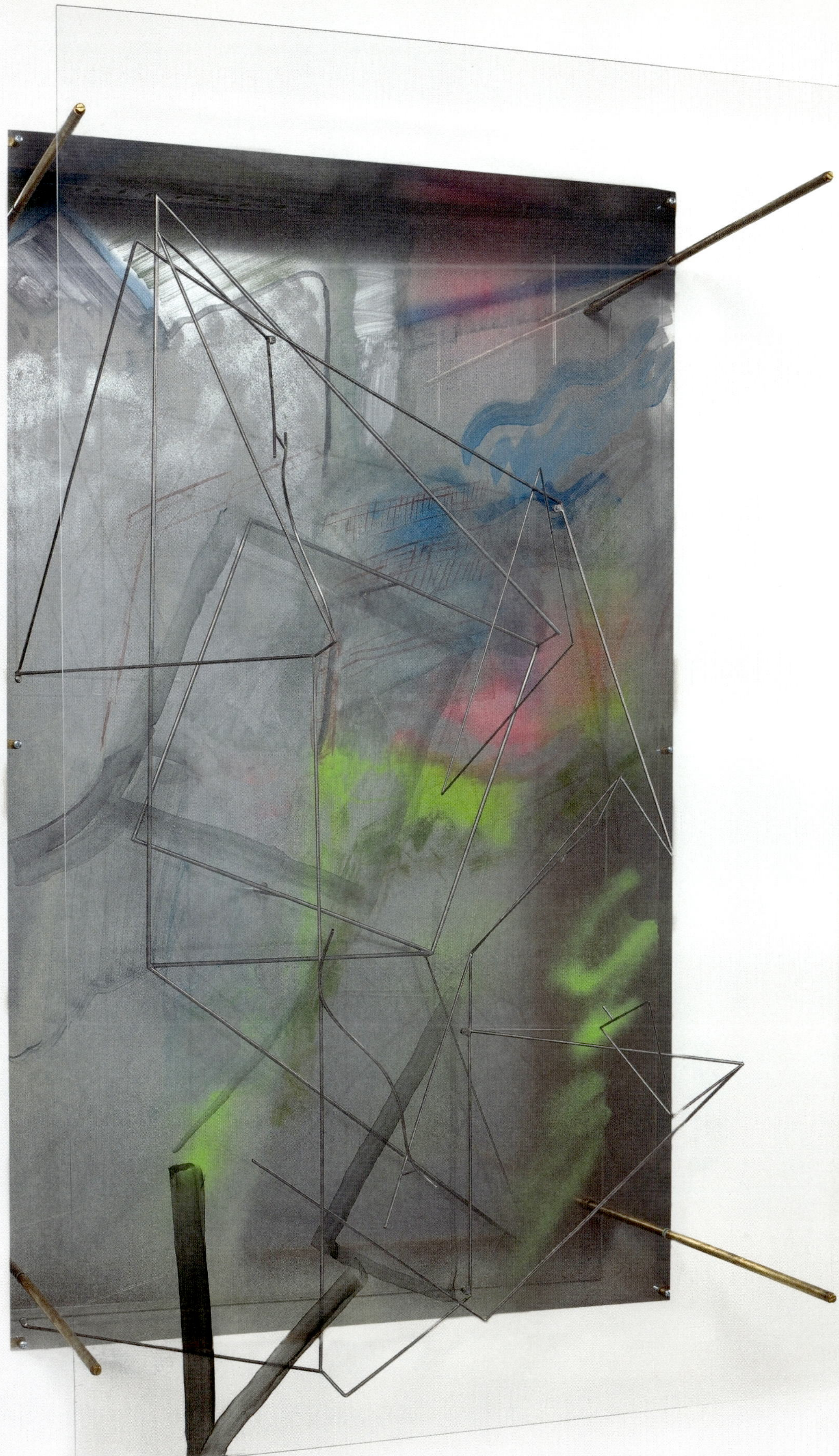

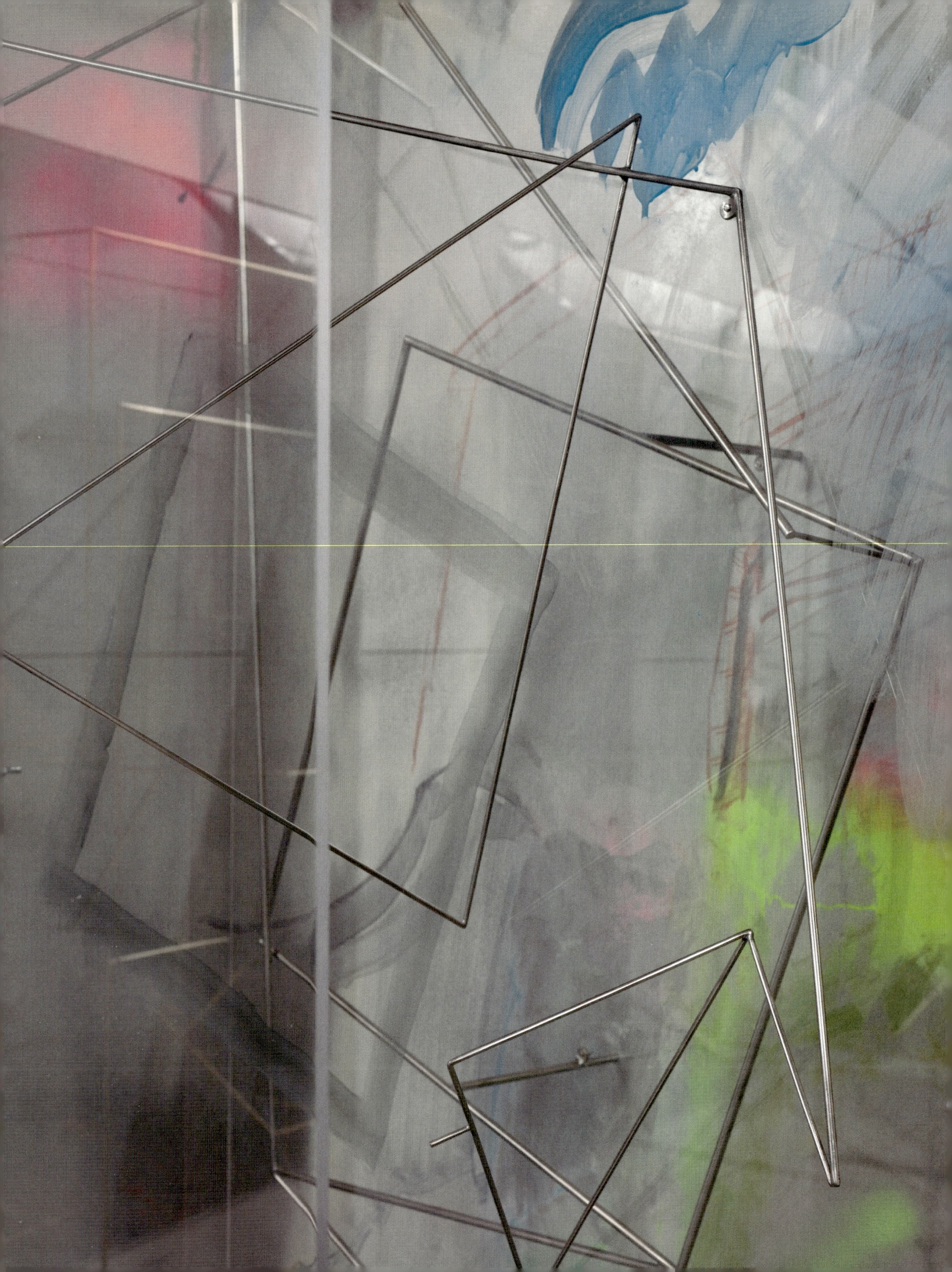

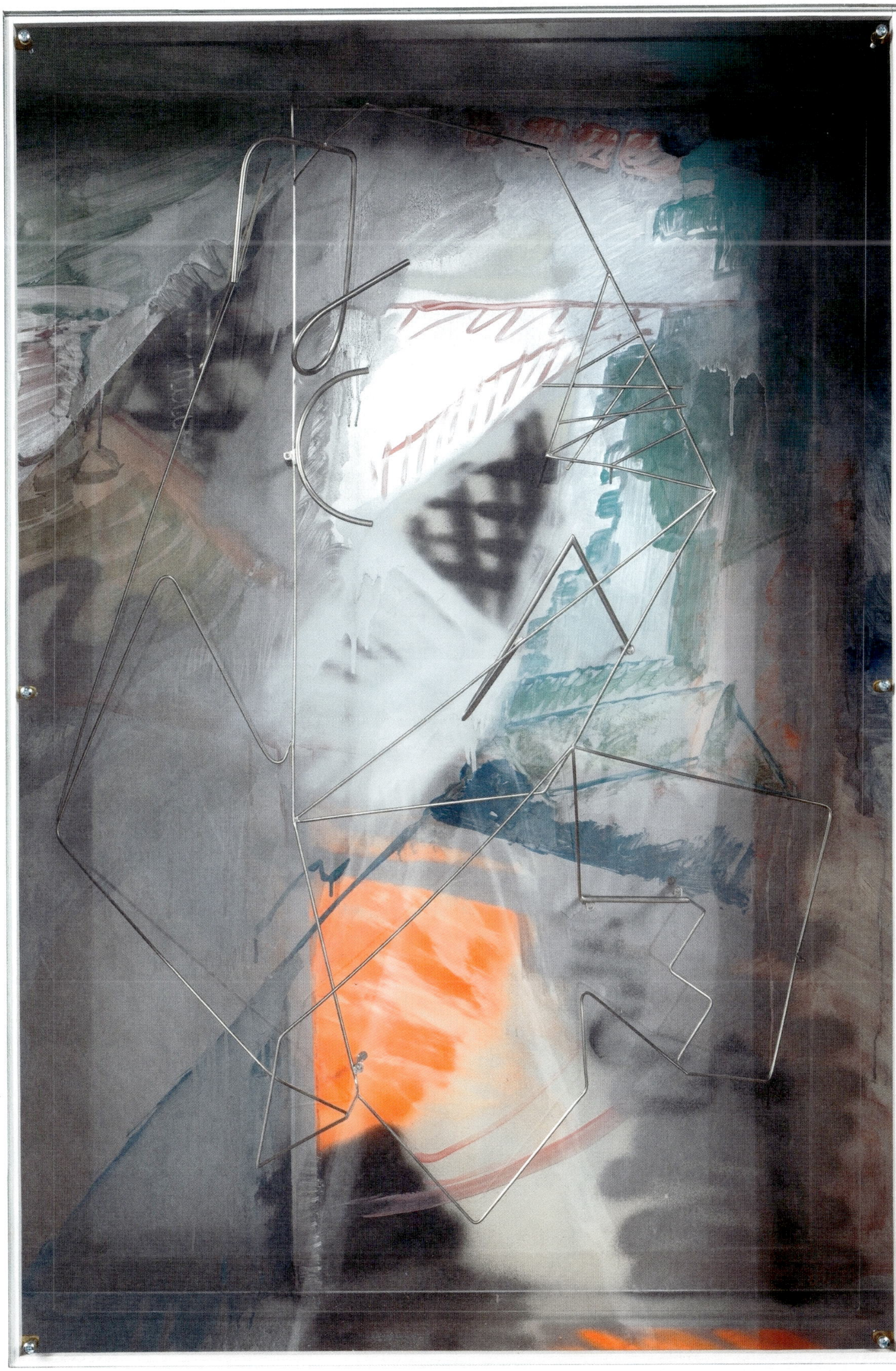

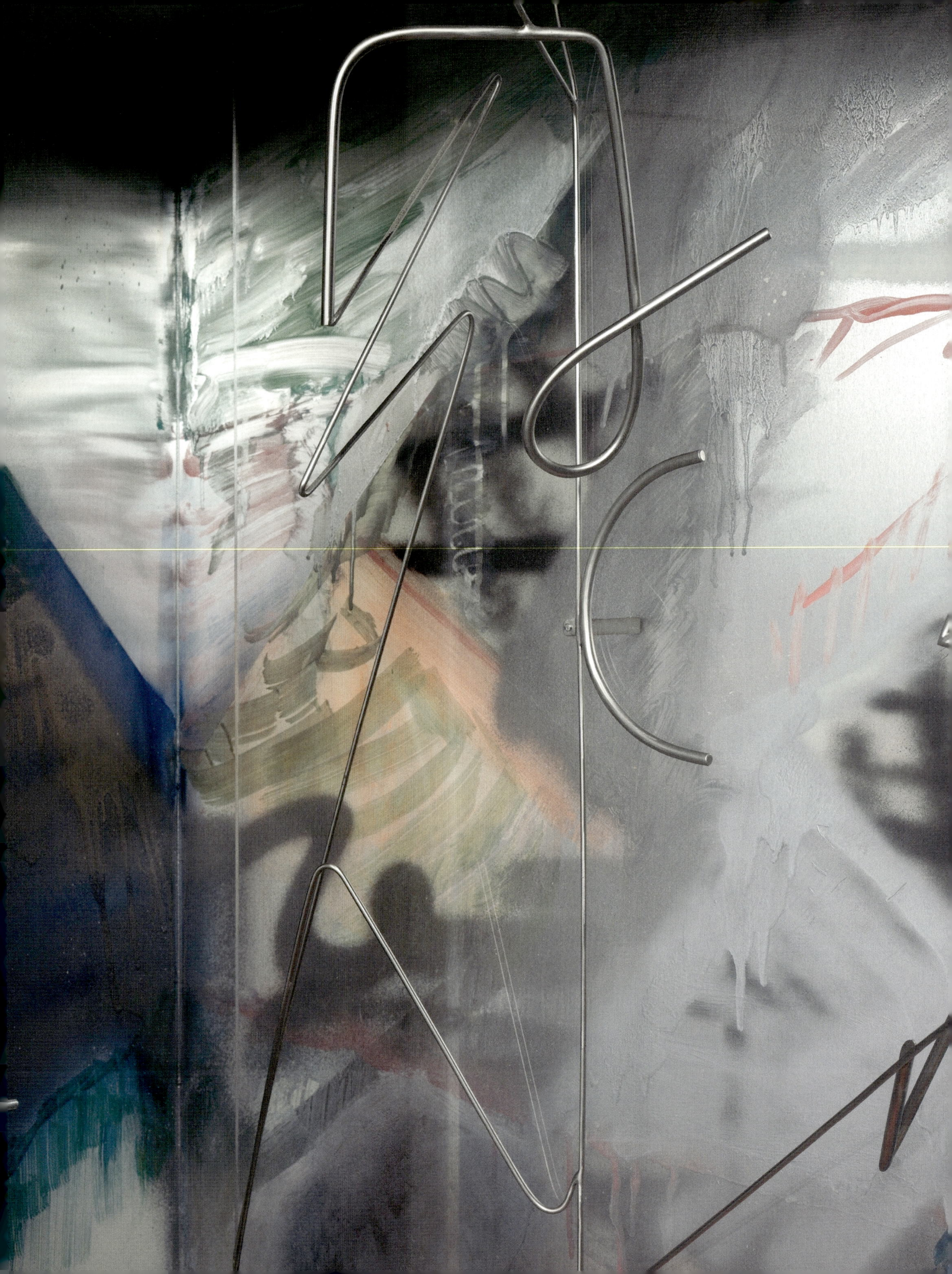

The Blue Woman
cardboard, concrete, acrylic paint,
wooden table-plinth

High Windows
concrete, paint, cardboard,
wooden table, wood filler

abject posture
clay, cement, cardboard, paint,
mahogany

unfolding arms behind my back
cardboard, cement, clay,
wood filler, acrylic paint, plywood,
mahogany

index finger traces the outline
steel, aluminium, oil paint,
gouache, grey filler, bolts

Salone
cardboard, cement, plywood,
acrylic paint

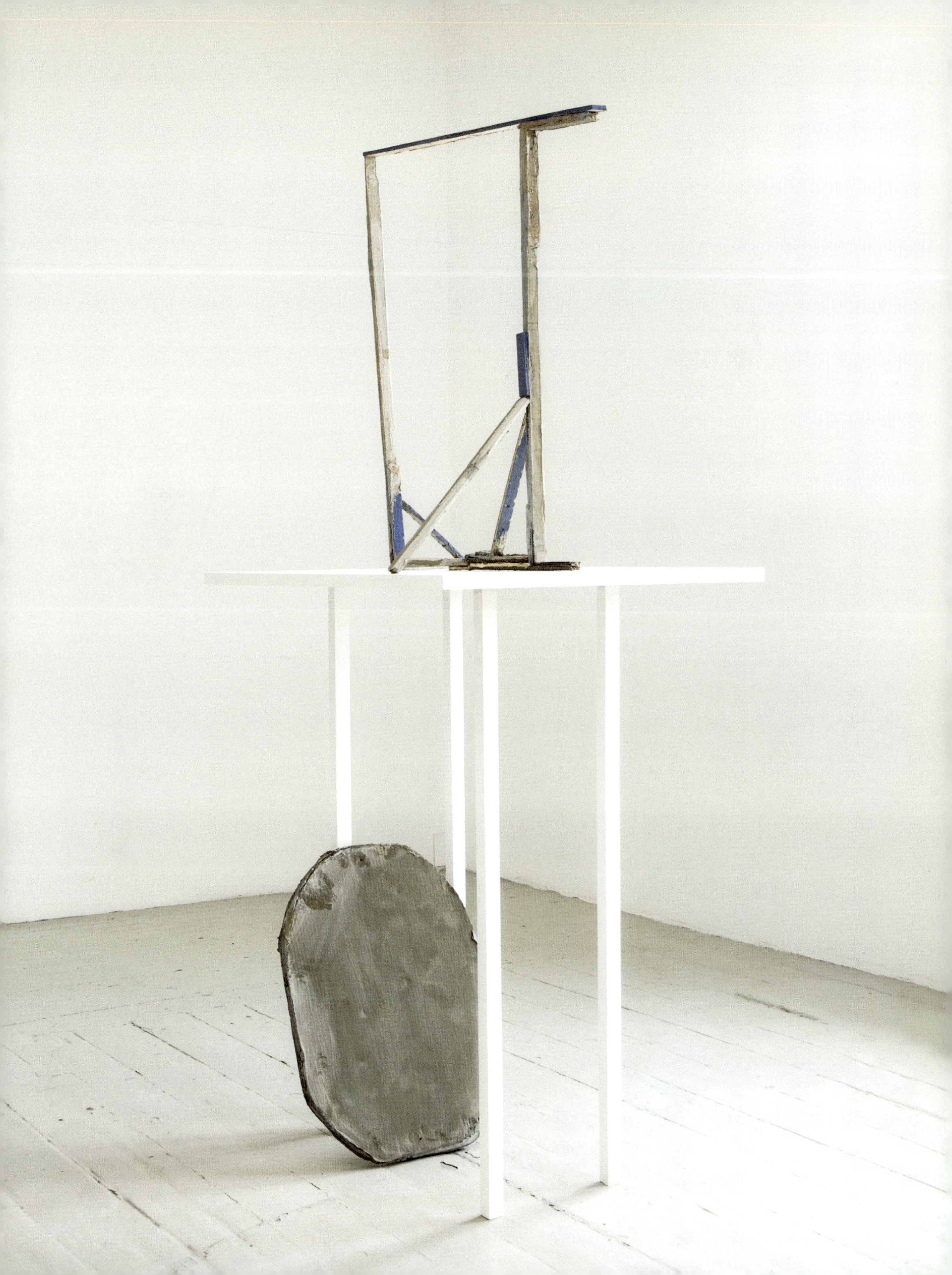

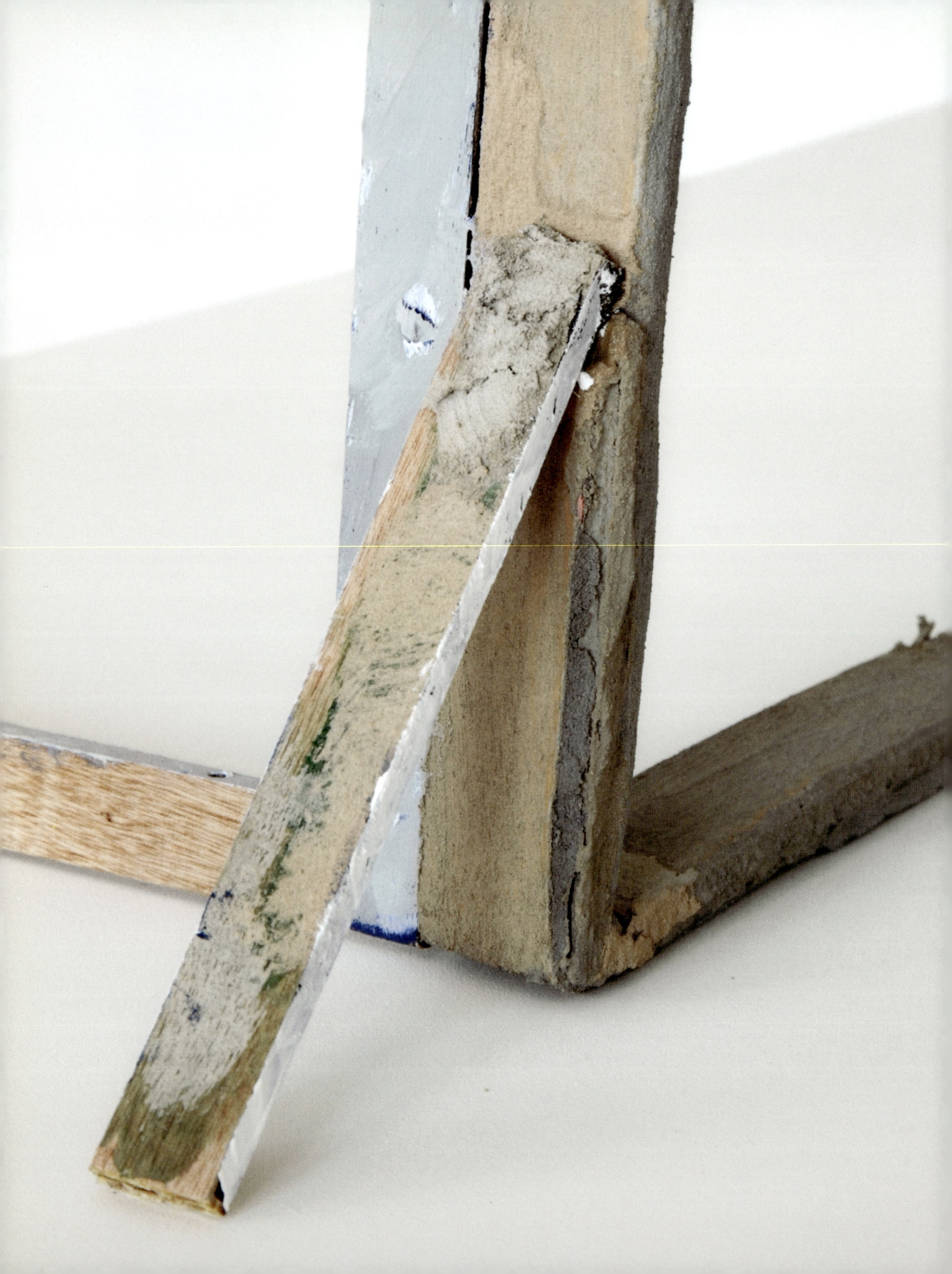

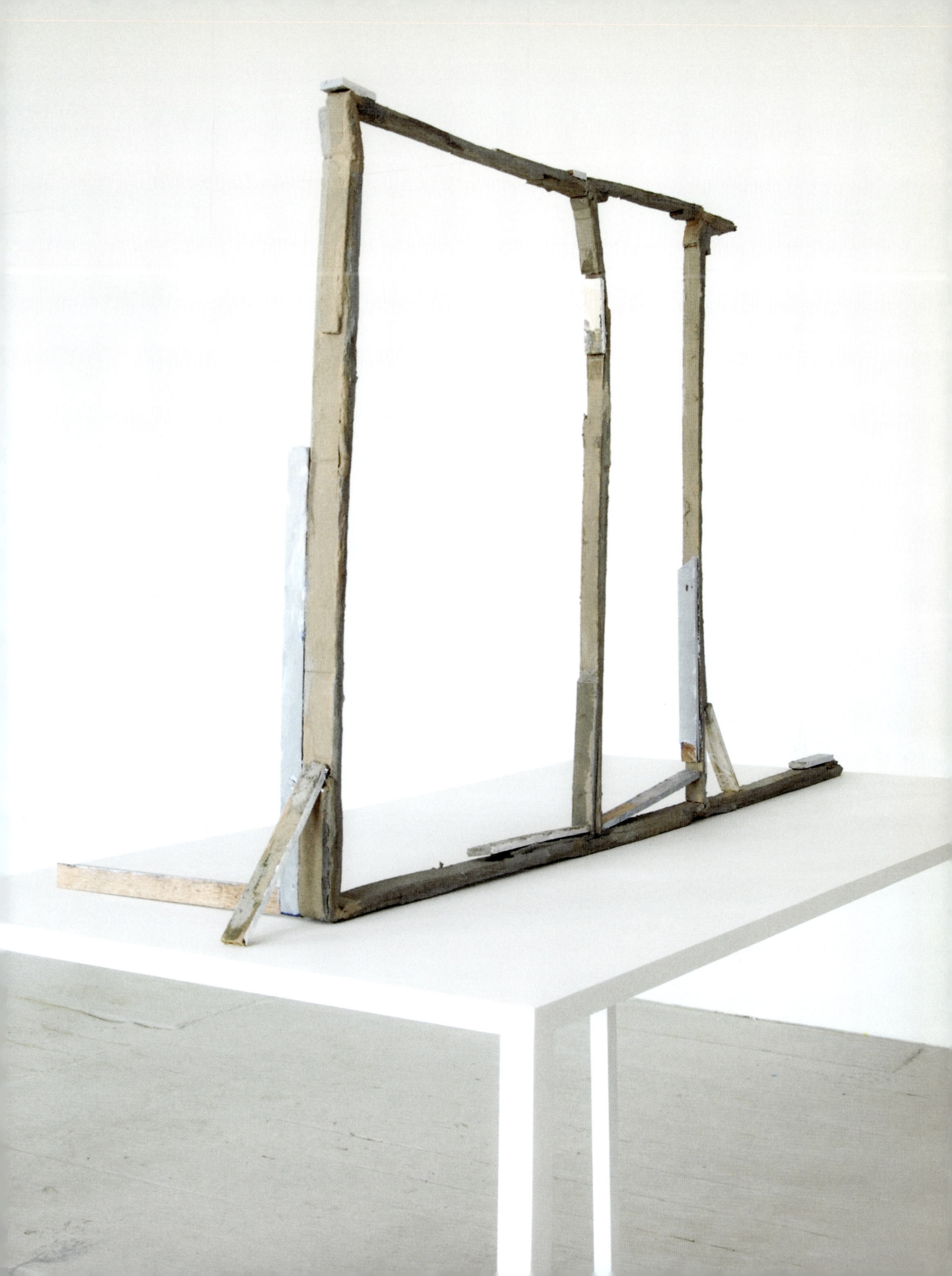

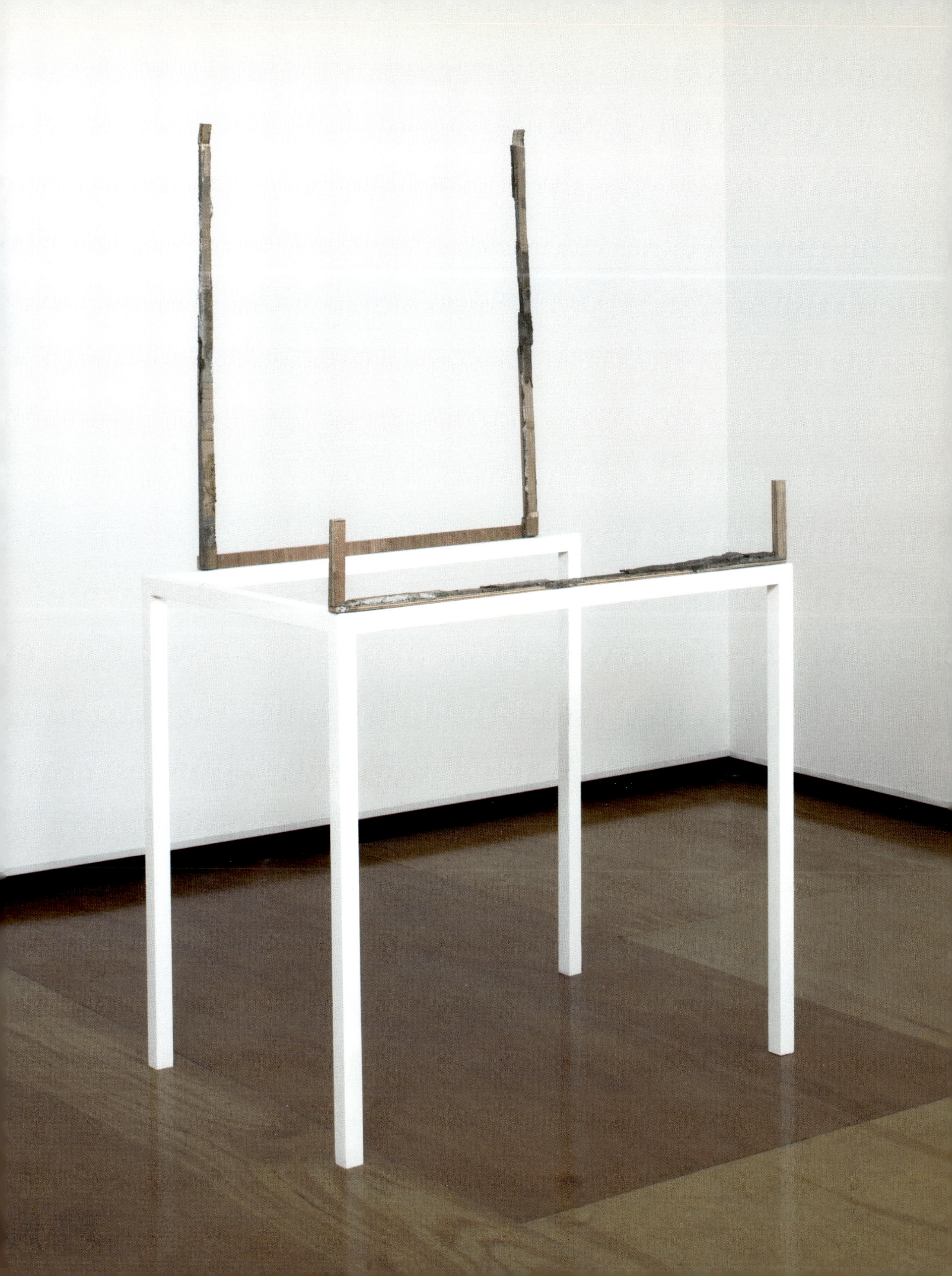

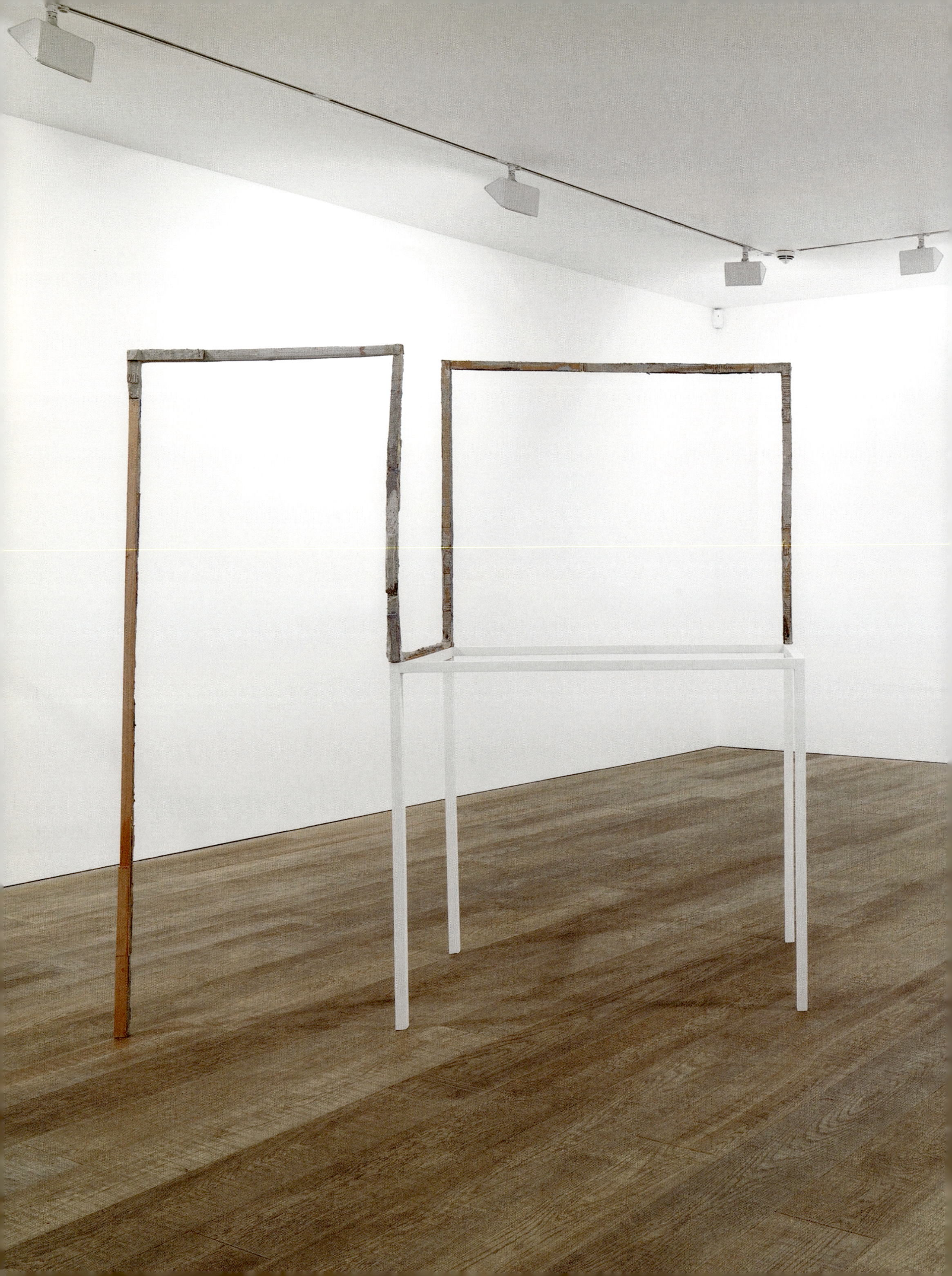

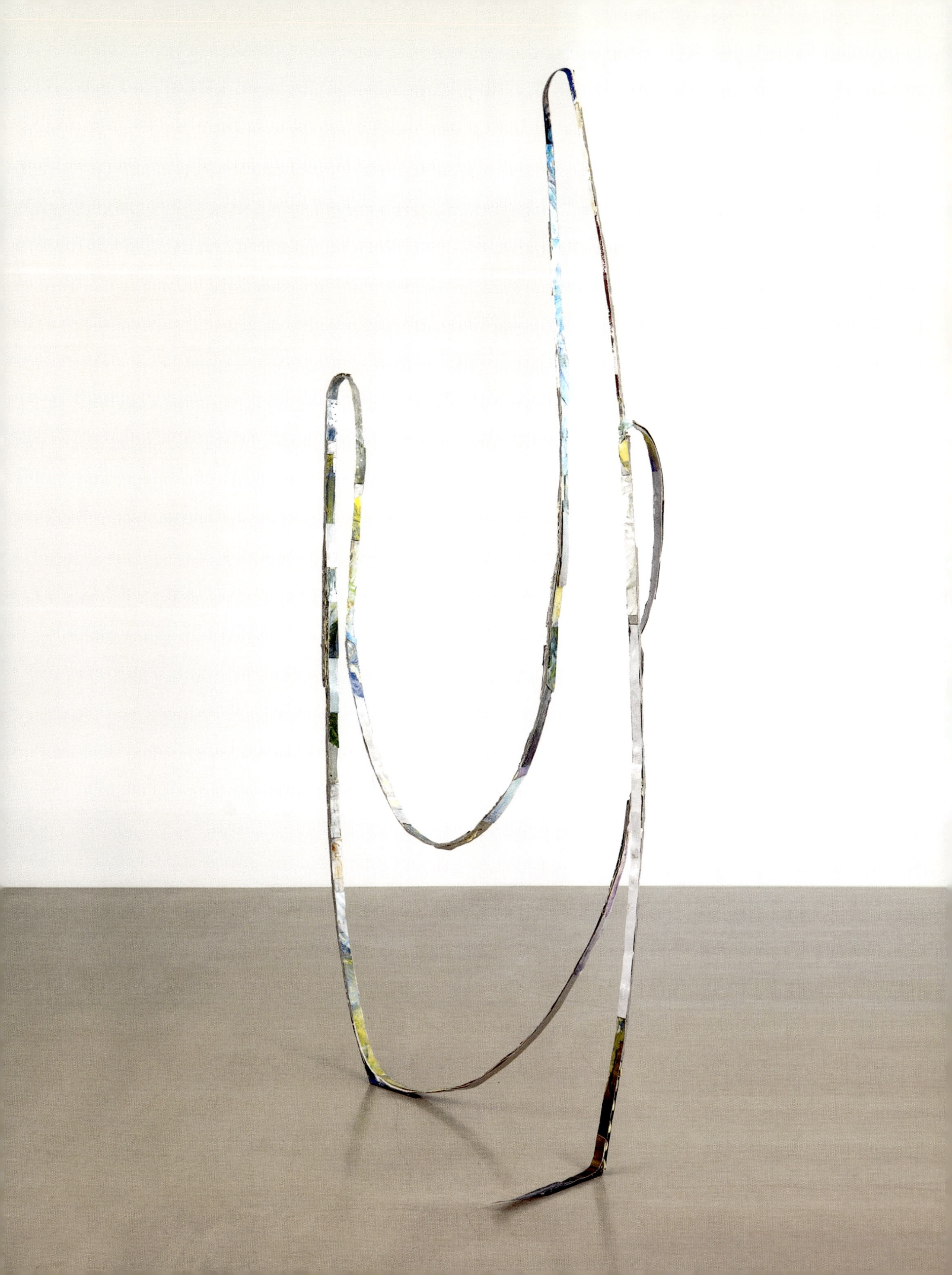

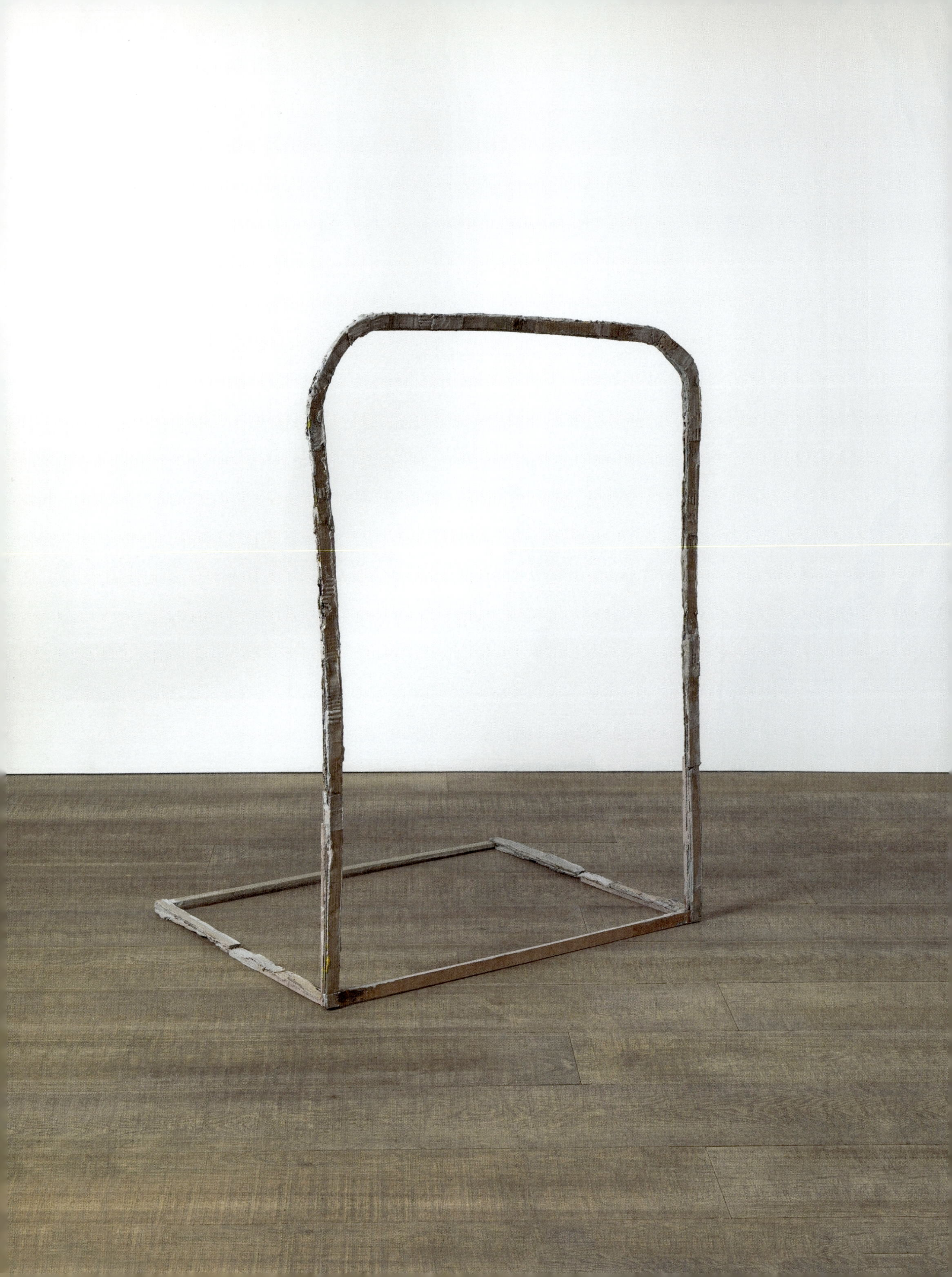

her point of view
steel, aluminium, various paints,
fillers, rivets

Fenestra
aluminium, gouache paint,
water-based primer, polyester
resin, glue on painted steel
and glass table

La Leçon de piano
aluminium sheet, oil based primer,
oil paint, polyester resin on glass
and steel table

washable colour
stainless steel round bar,
aluminium sheet, watercolour,
pencil crayon

story of a house
stainless steel round bar,
aluminium sheet, various paints

Watercolour seen
steel, aluminium, primer,
cardboard, grey metal filler,
watercolour, glue, rivets, bolts

representing a sketch
aluminium sheet, stainless steel
round bar, various paints

Woman at a Window
aluminium sheet, brass rod,
steel rod, balsa wood, acrylic
paint, gouache, metal filler

conversions
steel, aluminium, various paints

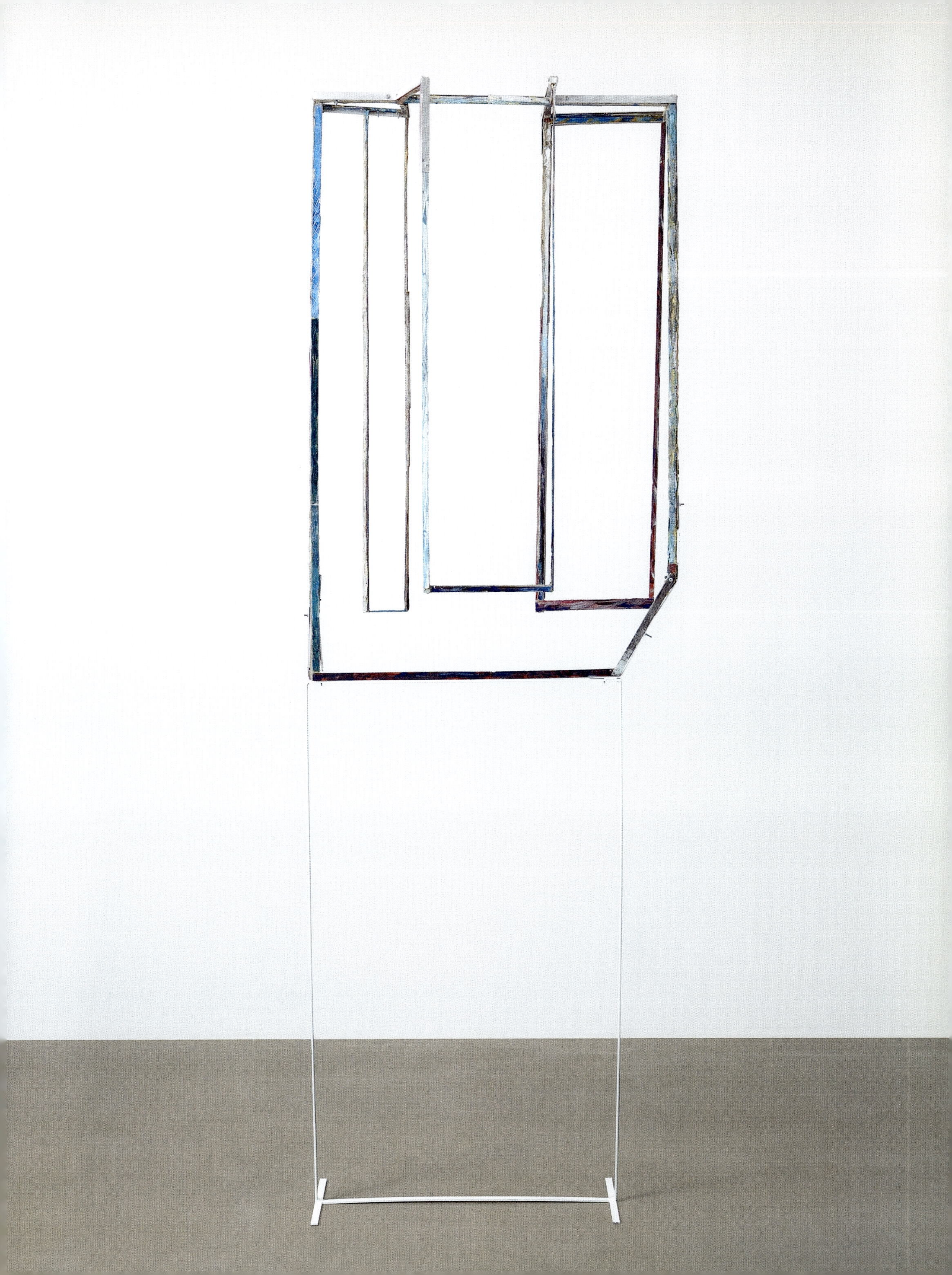

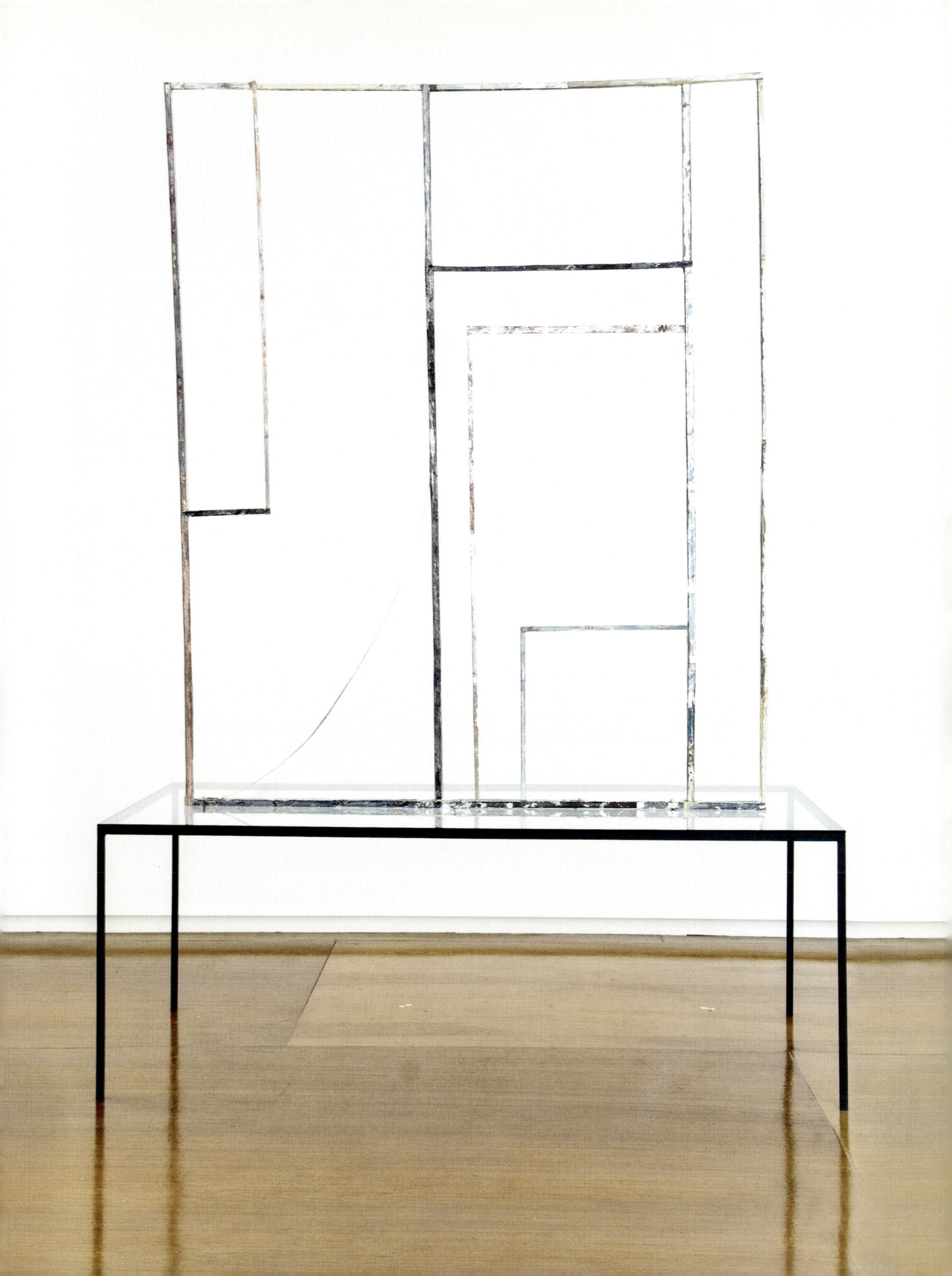

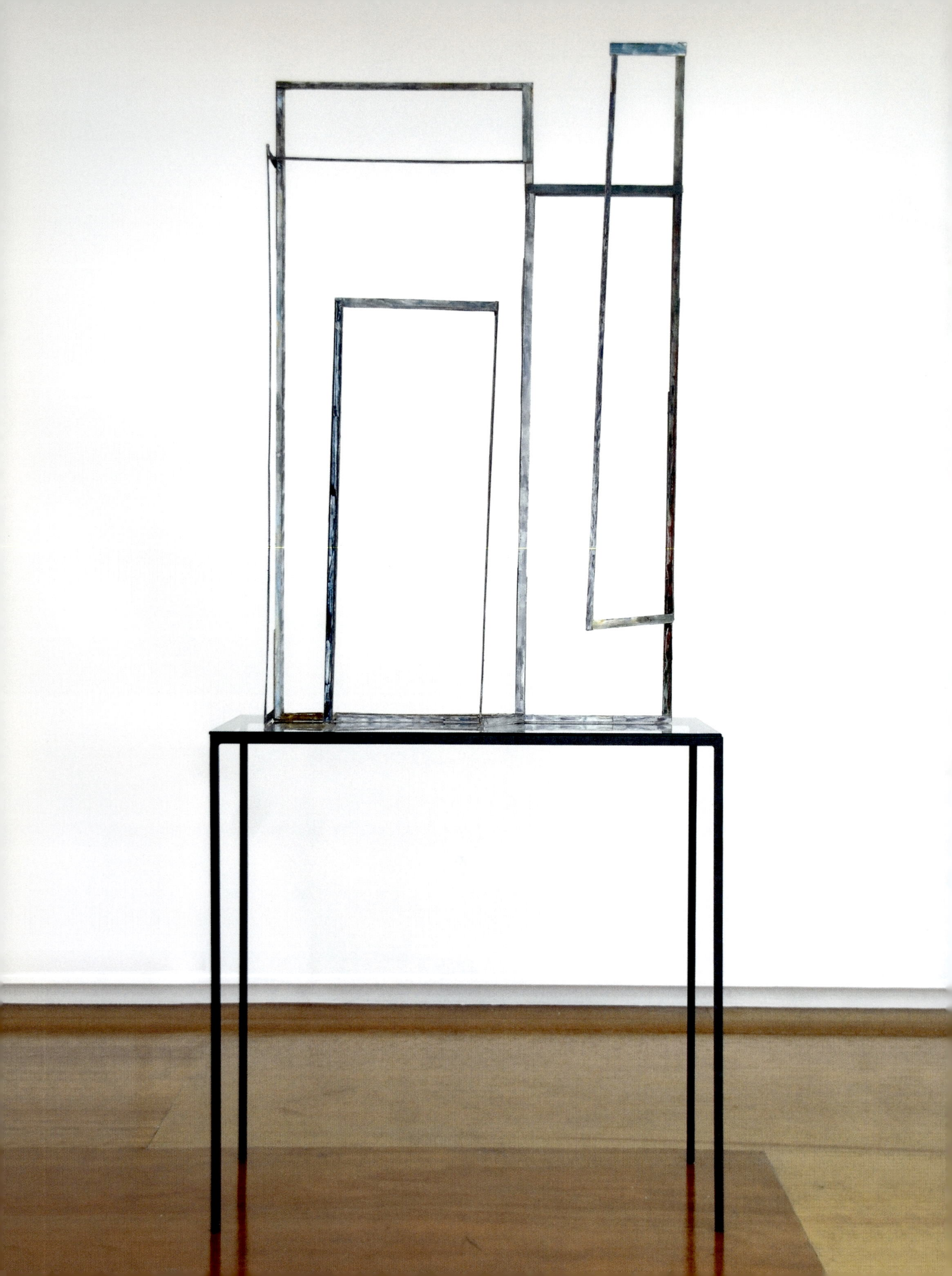

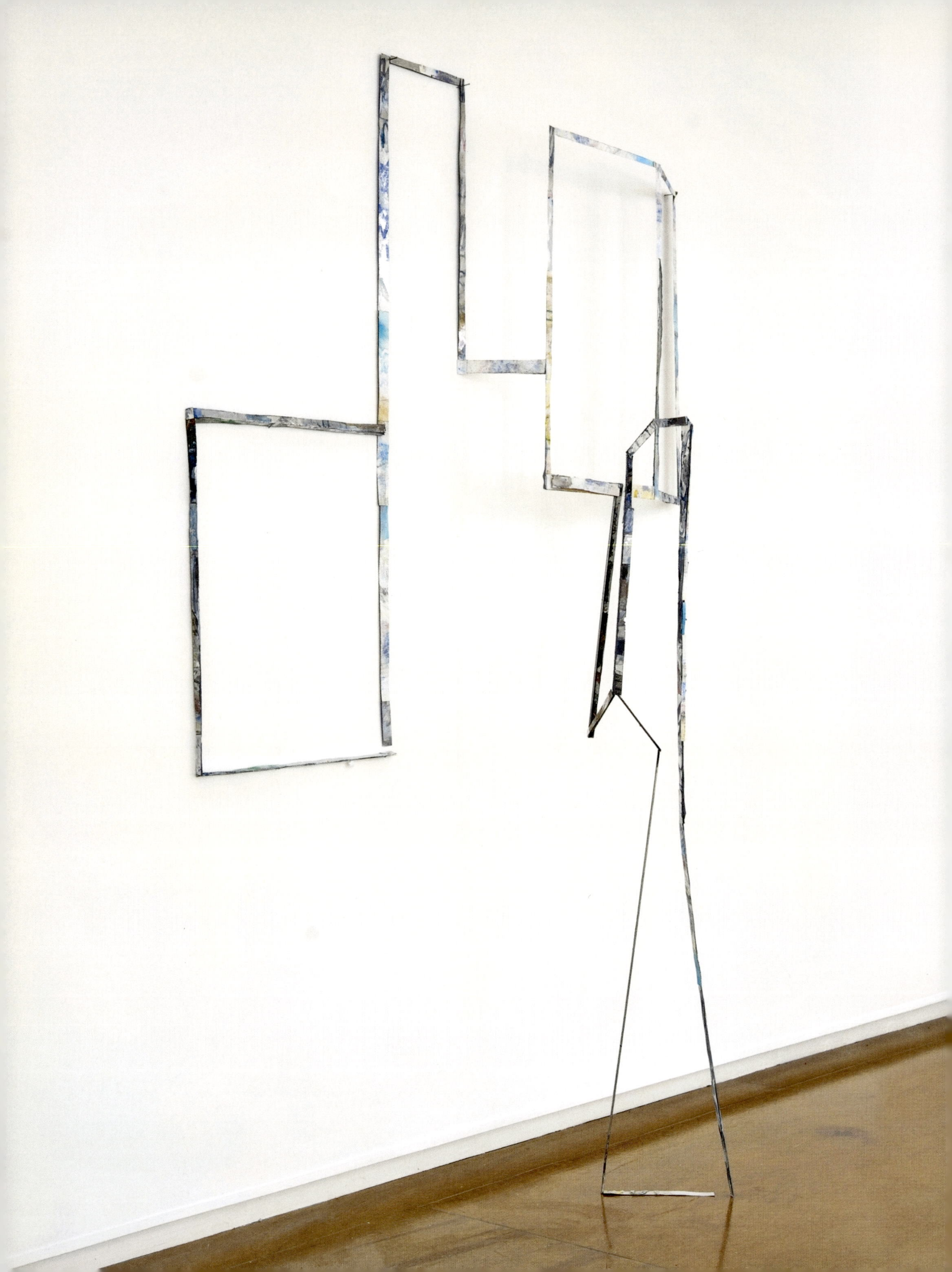

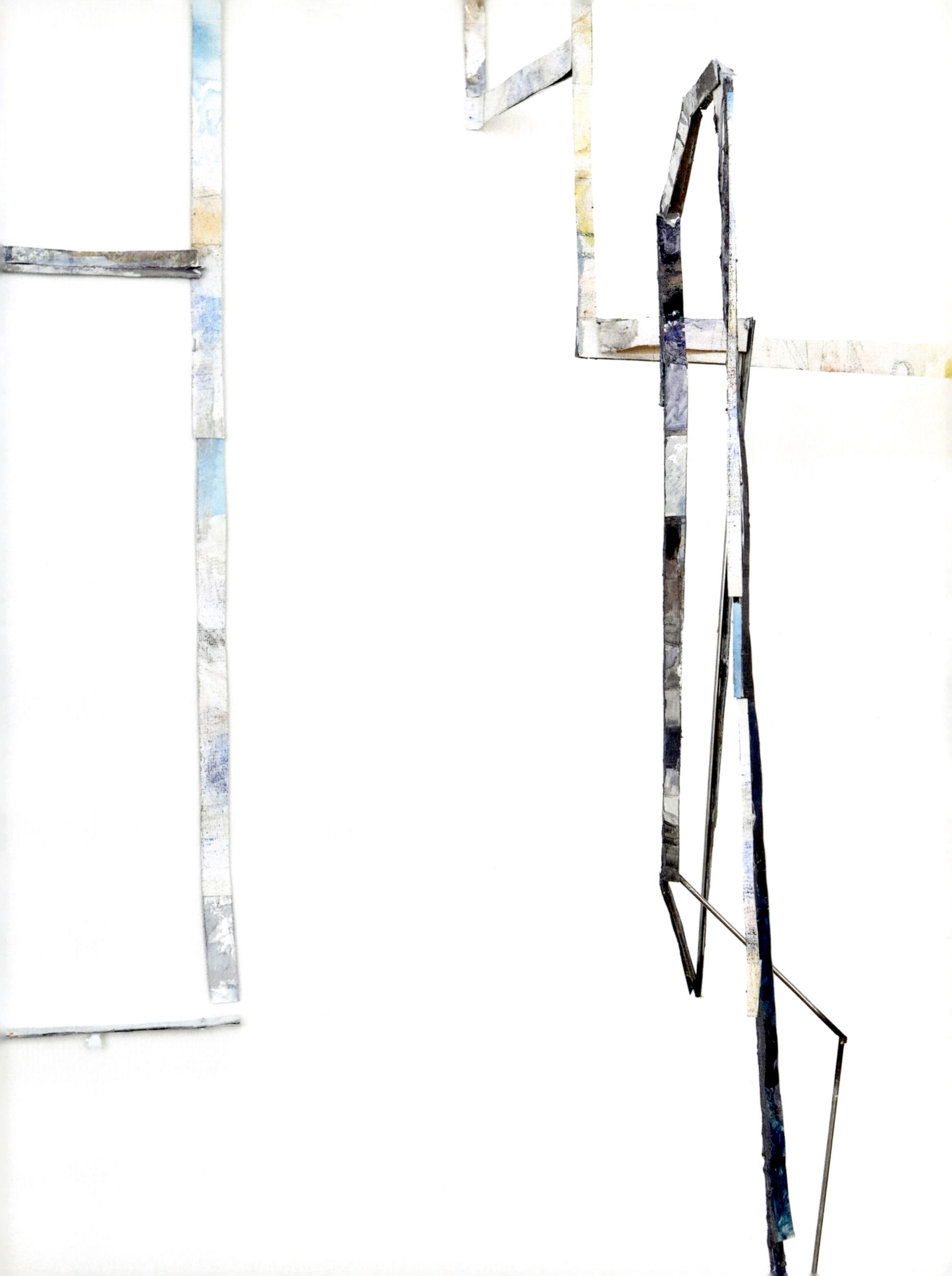

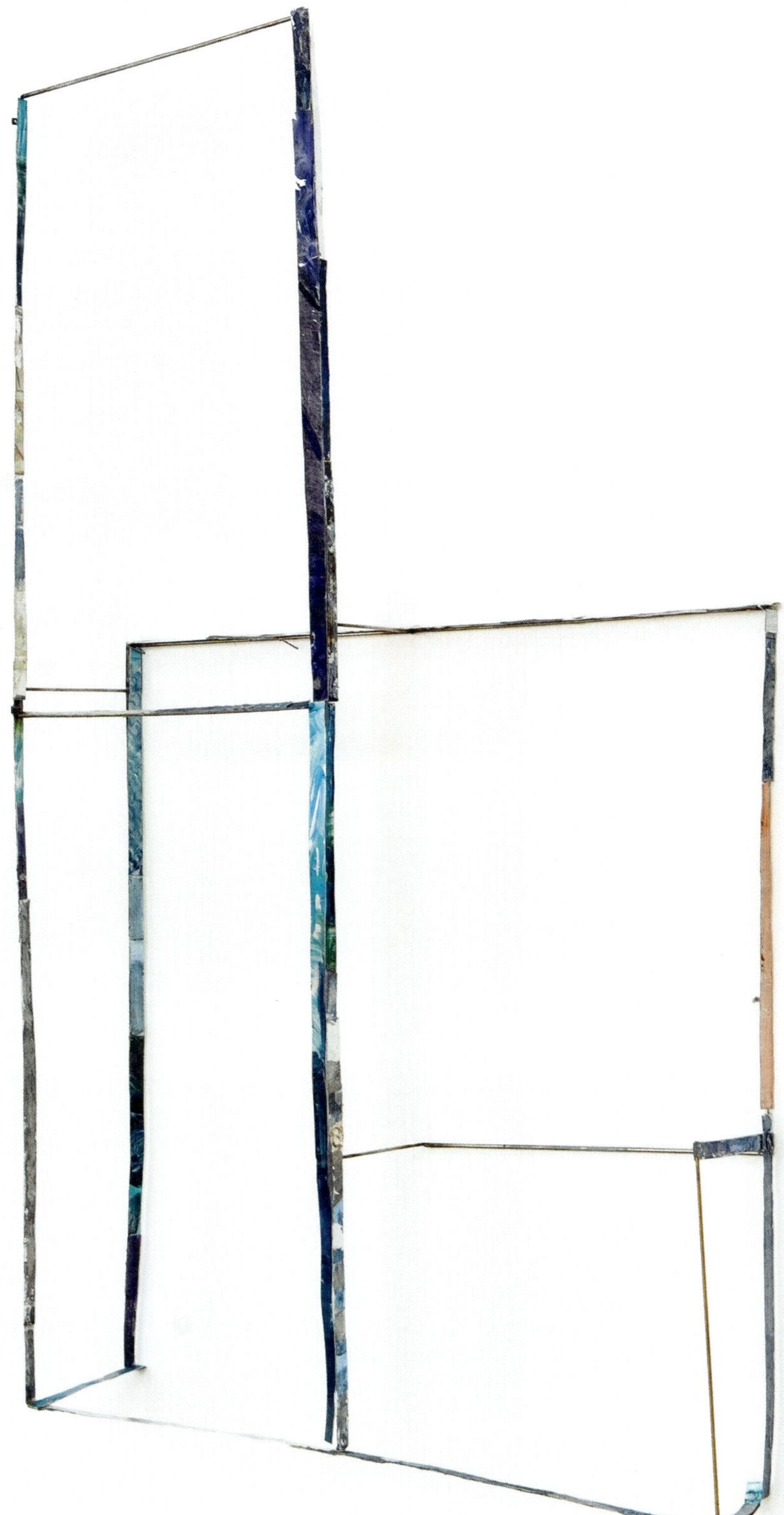

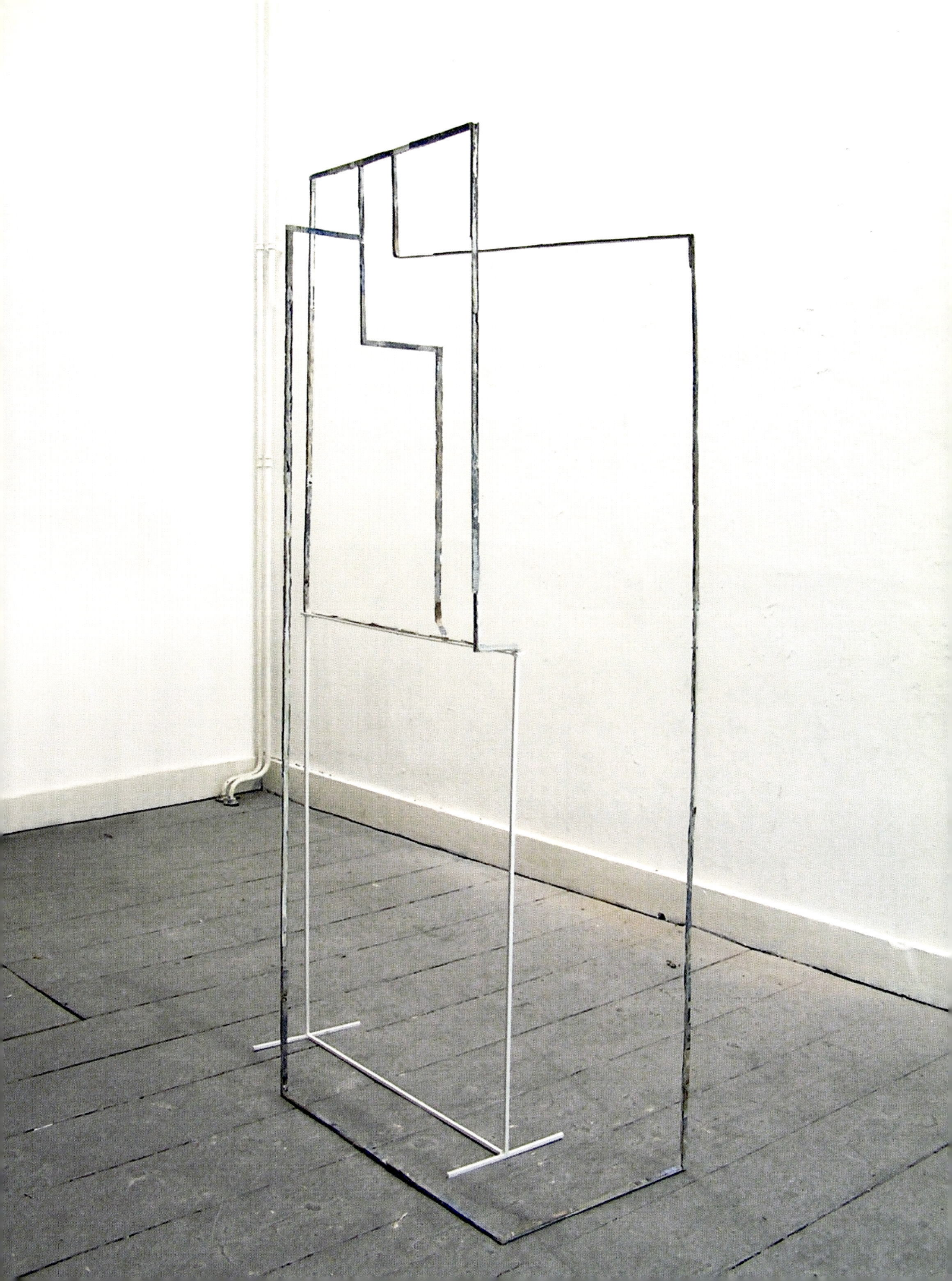

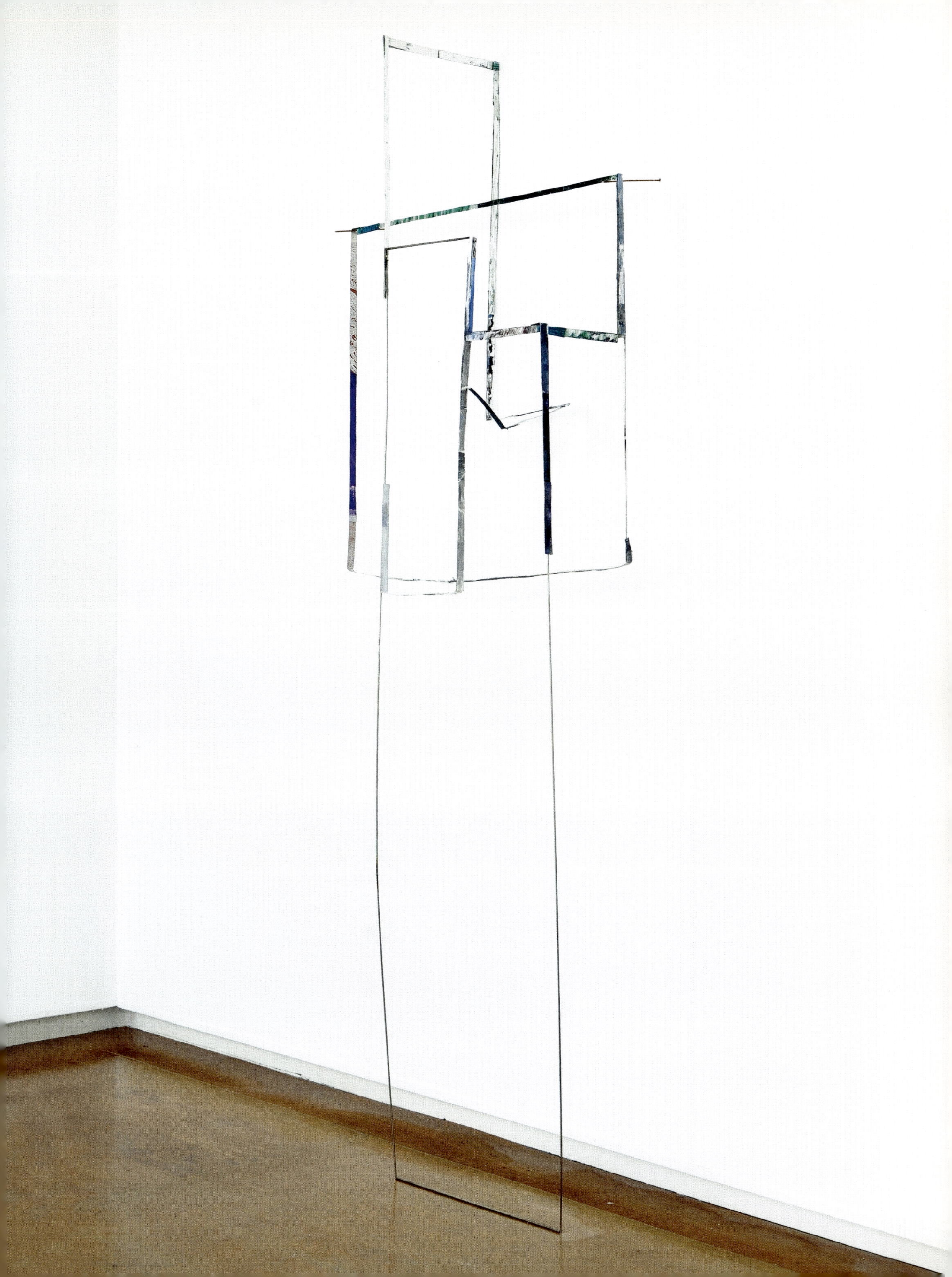

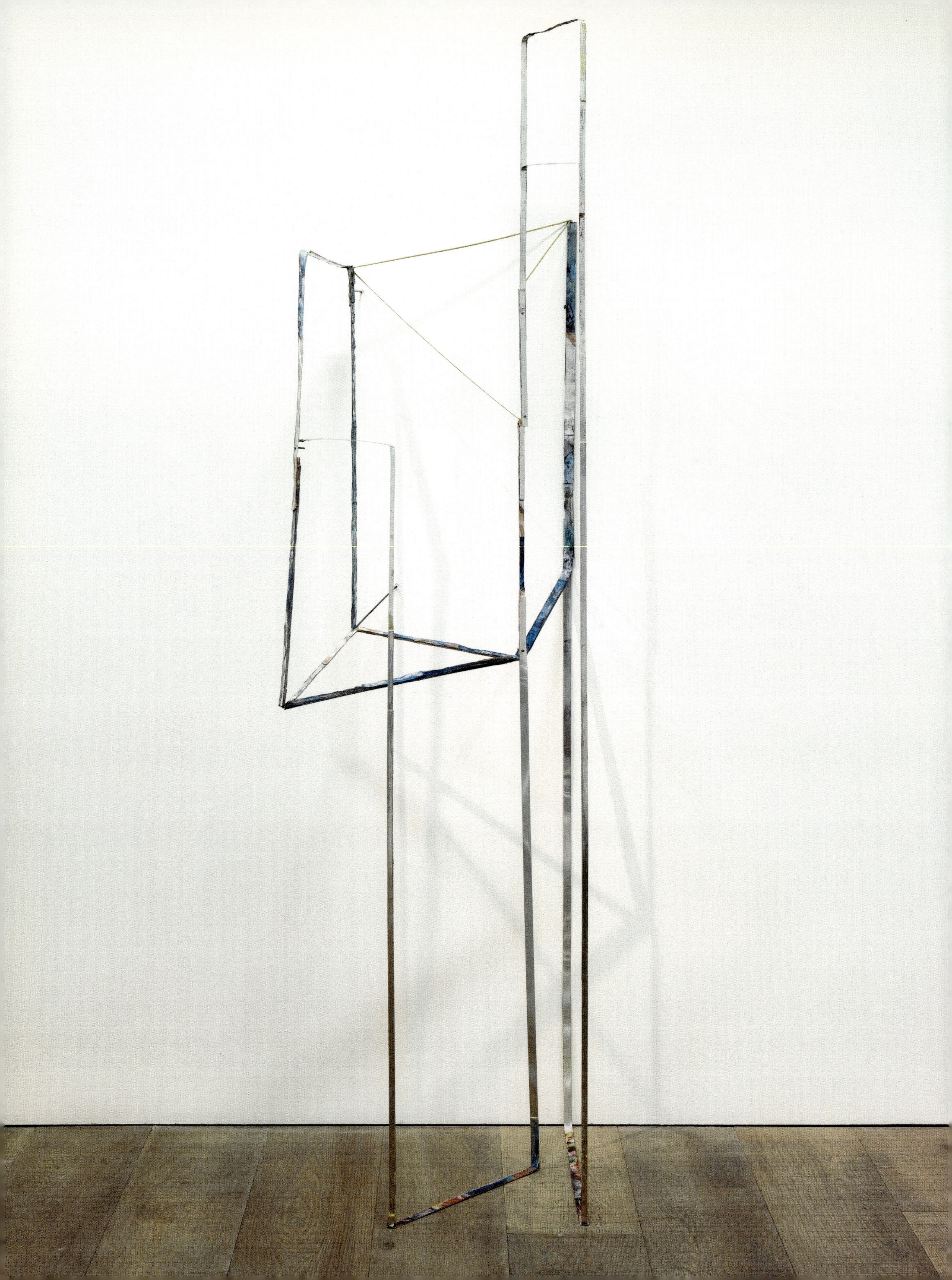

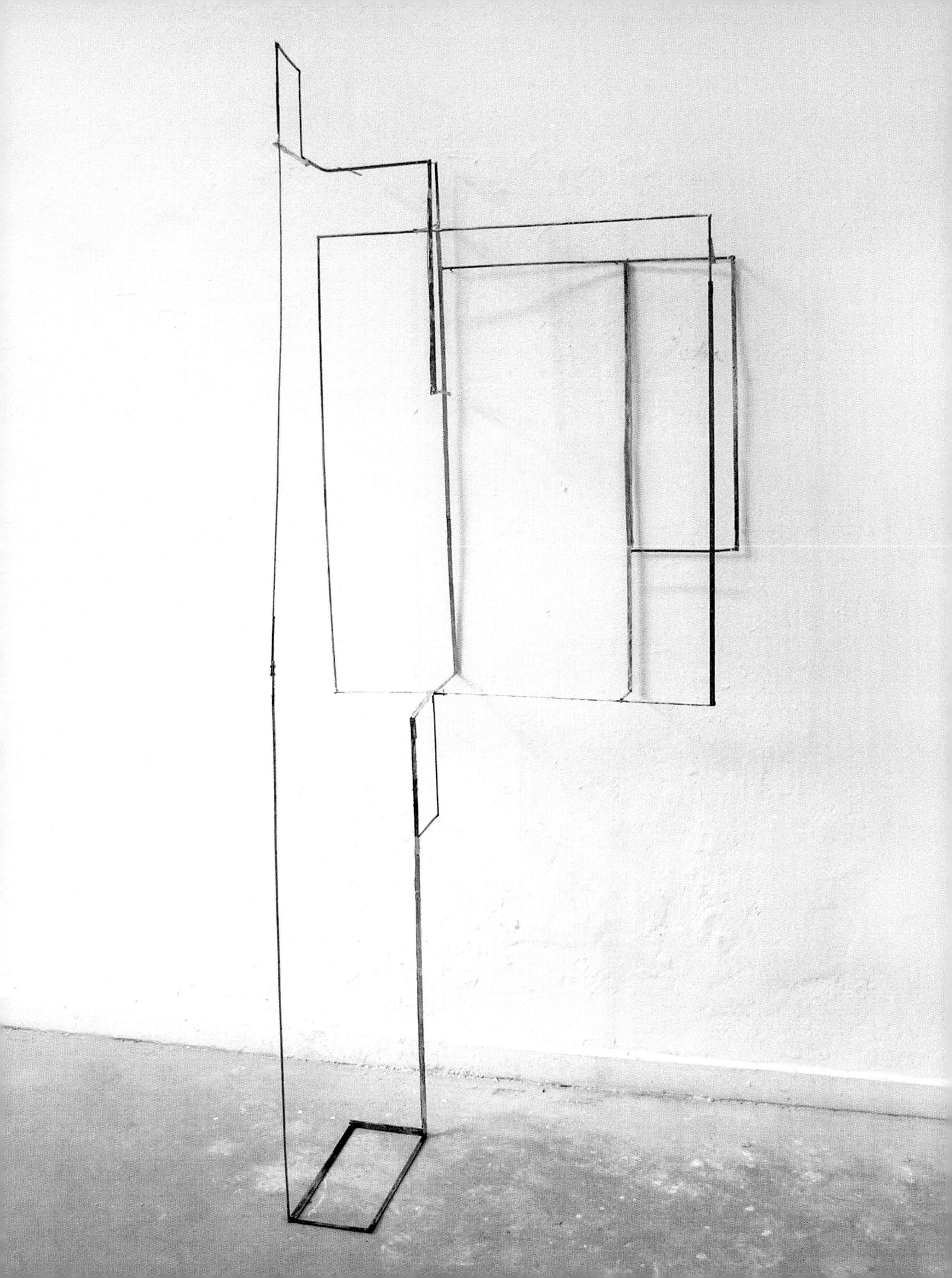

PRESENTNESS IS GRACE

KATHARINE STOUT

> ...she looked at the steady light, the pitiless, the remorseless, which was so much her, yet so little her, which had her at its beck and call (she woke in the night and saw it bent across their bed, stroking the floor), but for all that she thought, watching it with fascination, hypnotised, as if it were stroking with its silver fingers some sealed vessel in her brain whose bursting would flood her with delight, she had known happiness, exquisite happiness, intense happiness, and it silvered the rough waves a little more brightly, as daylight faded, and the blue went out of the sea and it rolled in waves of pure lemon which curved and swelled and broke upon the beach and the ecstasy burst in her eyes and waves of pure delight raced over the floor of her mind and she felt, It is enough! It is enough!
>
> Virginia Woolf, *To the Lighthouse*, 1927

The first half of Virginia Woolf's novel, *To the Lighthouse*, describes in delicious detail seemingly quotidian events as they unfold over the course of one day, centred around a house, a view, a group of people and how they connect to one individual, Mrs Ramsay. Offering a palpable experience of the everyday, it exemplifies the modernist quest to represent the present, the now, and prioritises the experiences, emotions, and thoughts of a woman caught between her duties and her loves, losses and personal longings. It exquisitely conveys the suspension of a moment, time slowed down and charged with a sense of trauma or pain yet to come, the revelation and implications of which are revealed in the second half of the book.

Sara Barker's works, in particular her early pieces, share many of the themes and interests in Woolf's seminal novel. For example Barker's recurrent interest in the boundaries of a room or personal space; the window as a threshold between an interior and exterior space; the gendered gaze; the physical and emotional ties between friends and family; and how we can simultaneously be intimate with those close to us and occupy a completely separate emotional and cerebral sphere. And in her non-figurative, mixed media works that optically flit between two and three dimensions, Barker also succinctly captures the psychological states that Woolf conveys. For example an emotive state of simultaneous presence and absence, that Barker's work achieves through its use of linear elements to create volume without mass, or the precariousness of a lived moment that is evoked through the apparent fragility and instability of interconnected vertical and horizontal elements. Barker's subtle deployment of mottled blues, greys, yellows and pinks to render the surfaces of her works echoes the very British palette of changeable sea and skyscapes, muted autumnal sunshine, wildflowers, and daylight fading into night that Woolf draws upon in her novels. Born in Manchester, raised on the Isle of Man (near the sea), and having lived in Glasgow for many years, Barker is sensitive to the myriad greys and blues of the city that can also suggest a view of sea or sky – or mood.

It is no coincidence that Barker's art has such affinity with Virginia Woolf – for her the solitary, intensely focused act of reading invariably accompanies and informs the making of a work. She comments, 'the reading comes at the same time – that energy that drives the work forward, gives it meaning, and at some point it comes together, you hope it comes together.' She is inspired mainly by women authors whose writing she particularly admires for the way it uses language to convey transitional states of being that can be described as both absolutely in the moment, and on the threshold of a life changing experience. For example, she comments, 'Jeanette Winterson writes really well about thresholds – to cross in and out is to enter different worlds, a transgression of our private co-ordinates, and allows for a shift in our assumptions that can be paradigmatic and lasting.' It is not only in novels that Barker finds the affect she is seeking – she reads also poetry, in particular Imagist poets such as Amy Lowell or H.D. As she describes, 'Imagist poetry, like Cubist painting, has that ability to synthesise multiple perspectives and bring them together to a singular vision.' Whether found in the modernist sensibilities of Woolf; or in the work of Imagist poets who sought to convey through a fragmented, yet precise use of language the significance of both the historic and individual time in which they were writing; or in the more recent writings of Winterson, Philip Pullman or Elif Shafak, Barker harnesses her intellectual and emotional response to specific texts to influence the composition, sense and visual tone of the work she makes.

Barker's work itself exists in a liminal space between media, in particular between sculpture, painting and drawing. The writer Jonathan Griffin succinctly captures the evasive nature of her work as it resists being categorised as one genre or another. 'The things that Sara Barker makes are less like sculpture than spatial drawings. Actually they're not so much drawings as paintings – surfaces for colour and brush marks, scraps of collage and daubs of textured filler. Then again, in their emphatic assumption of space, perhaps they are more like sculptures than paintings.'[1] In fact her work is imbued with the qualities of each of these separate disciplines: the surfaces are painterly and impressionistic; the delineation of the work is graphic and structural; and it exists in space with the same assurance as a figure. Yet her work occupies space in a manner that is hard to define: it resists boundaries and creates confusion. This characteristic can be traced back to a tradition of drawing in space, in particular the work of Julio González who in the late 1920s, in close dialogue with Pablo Picasso and his experiments with analytic cubism, deliberately set out to conflate drawing and sculpture by creating three dimensional works by welding together linear elements to create an impression of form whilst achieving a sense of weightlessness. However Barker, like her more recent predecessors such as Eva Hesse or Venezuelan artist Gego who have worked between drawing and sculpture, doesn't feel the need to categorise. Commenting on the relationship between drawing and her best known work, *Reticulárea* (1969), Gego's words seem equally applicable to Barker's work, 'The spatial conflicts are expressed in the same way in both genres. That's why I said it wasn't a question of drawing *Reticulárea* or of translating into two dimensions what the sculpture does in three. It is more about working with the same elements, space, emptiness and lines.'[2] Hesse constantly used drawing as a tool to reimagine sculptural language, exploring ways of connecting wall and floor as 'three dimensional drawing' in her notebook drawings from 1967, exemplified in a work such as *Hang Up* (1966) in which she literally took the line off the page, off the wall, and into space.[3]

Barker trained originally as a painter, and still sees her work as aligned with this discipline. In 2013, her work was included in a display at the Hamburger Bahnhof in Berlin alongside the work of Cy Twombly, another artist whose work offers a conduit between the visual and the literary, and whose practice encompassed drawing, painting and sculpture. Yet whereas Twombly's work invariably emits a Romantic grandeur with its gestural marks contained within the unifying ground of a large canvas, Barker's works have a more tentative, delicate sense of an object built up, or stripped back, through an accumulation of brushstrokes, lines balanced in space, materials juxtaposed and in support of each other. Each resulting piece is a self contained object, rather than a representation of an image or narrative. Barker describes how, 'There is an element of spatial painting, but I feel like I come at it from another direction. My natural instinct is for painting on bigger surfaces and then later there is a process of cutting away, editing, leaving sculptural remnants behind. It's a sort of backwards process, never conceiving of a sculpture, never drawing it first. But that process of drawing, the thin veneer between me and it has to happen whilst I'm making the sculpture.'

> It looked as if someone had cut a patch out of the air, about two metres from the edge of the road, a patch roughly square in shape and less than a metre across. If you were level with the patch so that it was edge on, it was nearly invisible, and it was completely invisible from behind. You could only see it from the side nearest the road, and you

> couldn't see it easily even from there, because all you could see through it was exactly the same kind of thing that lay in front of it on this side: a patch of grass lit by a street light.
>
> But Will knew without the slightest doubt that that patch of grass on the other side was in a different world.
>
> He couldn't possibly have said why. He knew it at once, as strongly as he knew that fire burned and kindness was good. He was looking at something profoundly alien.
> Philip Pullman, *The Subtle Knife*, 1997

In 2013, Barker was invited by the Baltic Centre for Contemporary Art to collaborate with Ryder Architecture to create a large work in one of the Baltic's double height galleries (pp.97, 98, 99). It was the first time she had partnered with architects, and through their conversations and practical consultations, Barker arrived at a work that is architectural in scale, but retains the provisional and seemingly spontaneous nature that can be found throughout her practice. She commented that she 'wanted a sense of play, association and reference to remain in the work, to 'stick to its surface'. The project allowed Barker to be more ambitious in her use of glass, an element that she has introduced into her work over the last few years to add another means of creating a play between a two dimensional flat image and a three dimensional volumetric object. She comments, 'The conflation between image and object has always been important in my work. Compressing the view to a series of images, reflects and fragments the form, relating back to the Cubist fragmentation that has been in the work before. This creates a sense of liminal disorienting of space – though the glass. The experience shifts moving around any three dimensional object, which is also a reason to make objects – to be surprised by them. The introduction of glass enables this interior and exterior world to be experienced at the same time, in that sense bringing back an idea that has been prevalent in the work, notional ideas of a sort of metaphor of the room, the boundaries of the room.'

The title of the Baltic work references *The subtle knife*, the second in a trilogy of books by Philip Pullman called *His Dark Materials*, which is premised on a world in which there are other dimensions and parallel worlds that are only accessible to some individuals. Barker says that Pullman, 'talks about a knife so sharp it can separate the membranes between one world and another. The book contains beautiful descriptions of bruise purples and sea blues, poetic descriptions of colour, which can guide the work as a starting point.' The book, which was mutually admired by and offered common ground between the architects and Barker, gives the viewer an insight into both the process and intentions underlying the piece. Barker describes how, 'I start with a more painterly process. What is left of the painting, slivers of aluminium, painted with gouache and acrylic, combination of materials. A suggestion of that other world, or like an opening, a cracked door – offering a glimpse of something through that editing process, leaving the most poignant part of a painting ... through that colour and mark-making, I feel that's a way for me to add this other layer of meaning, a more intimate sense of association can be brought to the work, stick to the surface of the work.'

The subtle knife's height and its use of shafts of glass, alongside rods of brass and steel that tower over the viewer, in contrast with Barker's usual anthropomorphic scale, create a slightly menacing impression that is further enforced by the title. Yet although the monumental scale required Barker to be more aware of the structural elements needed to support and stabilise the work, she was determined to retain a variety of more playful, and fractured elements, to keep the eye moving around the piece, and create a sense of inherent movement within it. She describes the elements that became important to her. Motifs of cross hatching, drawing or music staves, could slot in like drawing, to play off the two and three dimensional interpretation of the work. I wanted to find a rhythm with the branching, more fractal shoot-offs within the work. The glass, brass, steel and painted aluminium were dependent on one another – the glass is a support for the metal work, and the metal a scaffold for the glass. The glass creating transparent veils, creating volume. Compressing the work to a series of images.' The series of apparently floating plinths, used here for the first time by Barker, also deliberately undermines the weight and upward motion of the work, both giving it additional height and rooting it to the floor.

> I walk down the garden paths,
> And all the daffodils
> Are blowing, and the bright blue squills.
> I walk down the patterned garden paths
> In my stiff, brocaded gown.
> With my powdered hair and jewelled fan,
> I too am a rare
> Pattern. As I wander down
> The garden paths.
>
> My dress is richly figured,
> And the train
> Makes a pink and silver stain
> On the gravel, and the thrift
> Of the borders …
> Amy Lowell, 'Patterns', 1916

Commissioned in 2013 by Jupiter Artland to make her first outdoor work as part of the Edinburgh Art Festival, Barker set about her most ambitious use of glass, experimenting with ways for the work to both reflect and be a part of its natural setting. She comments, '*Patterns* (pp.101, 102, 104) is both here and not here. The glass allows it to disappear, despite it being heavier glass because of it being an outdoor work, but it somehow has a greater sense of ephemerality. The glass is so reflective that it complicates the image of it. It is, in a sense, a drawing in space as it has the fluidity of drawing. Although it is impossible not to evoke figuration, I find it more useful to think about the work as abstraction. In the sense that to be abstract is to be apart from concrete reality, not to make a fiction.' The prolific use of glass means that the lush green of the trees and foliage is incorporated as part of the work, and reciprocally the piece becomes a literal reflection of its environment. Barker selected the title after an Imagist poem by Amy Lowell, which is set on a garden path upon which a woman walks, having received news that her fiancé has been killed in battle.

In Summer 2015, Barker embarked upon another outdoor work again commissioned by Jupiter Artland, titled *Separation in the Evening (a celestial blossom before the yellow house* (pp.107,

108), after a 1922 Paul Klee painting. Comprising a greater number of painted elements than *Patterns*, the various metal and hand-painted surfaces create a collage of real and imagined landscape, where the rendered and reflected colour distorts and affects the perception of form. Like *Patterns*, the composition is continually shifting, responding to the different angles as the viewer moves around it, and according to the changes in seasons and environmental conditions, ensuring a singular comprehension remains out of reach. Barker's vocabulary of mark making with paint draws on various influences, including Klee's version of pointillism in which he built up form and imagery through dots of colour, but also encompassing the Japanese prints of Utagawa Hiroshige, a nineteenth century Japanese master of *ukiyo-e*, a form of fluid image making that shares a kinship with drawing. Barker comments on this work, 'I'm always trying to use the elements of construction in less familiar ways, to pair the materials of industry with softer polished brass and painted surfaces, to form what is essentially a painting in space. The heavier materials of industry and the more refined processes of silversmithing are combined to make a work for outdoors that remains delicate and jewel like.'

> I become almost a shadow
> The kind that extends up the wall,
> Across the ceiling,
> Dwindled gradually into other shadows.
> In my room.
> Theirs.
> Ann Quin, 'Three', 1966

Over the last couple of years, Barker has begun to introduce black and white backboards into her work to explore further the relationship between figure and ground, in particular an exploration of surface and shadow. In her exhibition at carlier | gebauer, Berlin in 2014, titled *I become almost a shadow*, Barker juxtaposed wall based works that operated as 'reliefs'(in that the sculptural elements were set against a background plane) with three dimensional works that stood in the centre of the space, their elements framed against horizontal plinths that seemingly floated above the ground. This enabled Barker to see how these pieces – or characters, as she describes them – operated in conversation with each other. The black background flattens the image, bringing the sculptures closer to the realm of drawing, or painting upon a flat surface, especially as the dense black soaks up any light or reflection, thereby refuting the shadow and giving an impression of immense depth. In contrast, the cast shadows are an instrumental part of the freestanding pieces, an almost kinetic element that moves and mutates as the viewer moves around the works, emphasising their linearity. Barker describes how she was thinking about these two different modes of viewing, and the shifts between them whilst conceiving the exhibition, wanting to explore a 'consciousness of being viewed – and being a viewer. There is somehow a psychological space, a sense of darkness. Trying to set up a sense of character in the space, a narrative, or some kind of plot between these characters, i.e. the sculptures, in the space.'

> I am writing for myself and strangers. This is the only way that I can do it. Everybody is a real one to me, everybody is like someone else to me. No one of them that I know can want to know it and so I write for myself and strangers.
> Gertrude Stein, *The Making of Americans*, 1906–8

The setting up of a series of dialogues between works, between horizontal and vertical planes, between the second and third dimensions, between the practices of drawing, sculpture and painting and between the architecture and the volume of the space all informed Barker's approach to her exhibition at the Gallery of Modern Art in Glasgow, also in 2014 (pp.117, 118–119, 120, 123, 124, 125, 127, 129, 130). The conversation between abstraction and representation, whether of a real, observed reality, or an imagined world, is also very pronounced in the body of work Barker made for this exhibition. These concerns are set against an exploration of a subjective narrative that appears to underlie all the works, without being brought to the fore. Barker describes how the title, *for myself and strangers*, was, 'named after the way Gertrude Stein used to describe her writing, to get across the difficulty of knowing how people perceive your work, or being able to predict this. So in many senses she was making work for herself.' It is noteworthy that Stein was a contemporary, and indeed personal friend of Picasso and the other Cubist artists, and the way her writing captures multiple viewpoints is exemplary of the early modernist writing that Barker looks to as an equivalent for what she is seeking in her own work.

Another influential artist of the early twentieth century whom Barker cites as an ongoing inspiration is Paul Klee, an artist whose experiments with abstraction sat independently from those of his peers. His 1920 statement, 'Art does not reproduce the visible, rather, it makes visible',[4] eloquently captures Barker's own ability to embody rather than simulate an emotion, experience or thought. Barker relates her use of the blackboard to the influence of Klee, 'In later works, I have started to introduce these blackboards. In some works they shift the way you see the space, not unlike the huge black canvases of Paul Klee, whom I look at a lot. They play with a sense of depth of the space, flatten the space ... so the forms wouldn't necessarily have to reference becoming figurative, but could be purely these symbols or motifs and closer to the painterly influences in that way. This is the direction the work has been going in – to be dealing with pictorial space, maybe out of finding a frustration with that editing out and wanting to explore the picture frame a bit more.'

This shift to a pictorial space is evident in the large scale work *HOURS BECOME HANDS (Foliage of Palms)* (2014, pp.124, 125). In this work, Barker literally drew out the studio environment with the filigree metal work that sits against the black background, acknowledging in the title of the piece her long interest in Matisse's cut-outs and interiors.[5] She comments, 'The idea of bringing a notion of space/creative space/personal, biographical space into the gallery is subtly important. The hands wrap around the wall, back and front.' Another major work, *The Human Family* (2014, p.127), this time set against a white background instead of black, also invites a descriptive reading, though the angular forms are definitely not figurative in a conventional sense but are perhaps reminiscent of the language of Orphism, or Orphic Cubism, which focused on pure, often geometric abstraction as an sequential offshoot from Cubism. Barker's personal life and familiar environments offer a direction for the works in this exhibition, which may be a response to it being her first major exhibition in her hometown. Perhaps it is also no coincidence that Barker was pregnant at the time of preparing for the show, itself a strange liminal time, in which the body is already nurturing, caring for a person as yet unknown – for all intents and purposes the stranger of the exhibition title.

> I am suggesting, then, that a kind of latent or hidden naturalism, indeed anthropomorphism, lies at the core of literalist theory and practice.

> The concept of presence all but says as much, though rarely so nakedly as in Tony Smith's statement,
> 'I didn't think of them [i.e., the sculptures he 'always' made] as sculptures but as presences of a sort'...
>
> We are all literalists most or all of our lives. Presentness is grace.
> Michael Fried, *Art and Objecthood*, 1967

Michael Fried's influential text, *Art and Objecthood*, written at the height of a late modernist movement self-defined as centred on a New York School of painting and sculpture, poses a conundrum in that it is explicitly negative about what Fried describes as a theatrical turn to literalism in sculpture, yet is highly perceptive in defining the innovations of the new sculpture being made, characteristics that went on to influence future generations. What Fried saw as an inappropriate focus on the circumstance in which three dimensional work of art is encountered – an emphasis on an anthropomorphic 'presence' that demands a reciprocal relationship with its viewer – remains highly regarded today. Barker's works always require an active, empathetic conversation with the viewer, not least because they cannot be optically read, but must be experienced in the round. They embody a compelling personal space akin to another figure, often emphasised by their human-size scale, and the complexity of their three dimensional forms. Yet they do this through a contradictory lightness and fragility, due to the thinness and delicacy of the component elements that speaks of the vulnerability of our emotional selves.

NOTES

All quotes from Sara Barker are taken from a Culture Now talk, ICA, London, 21 February 2014 or from email correspondence with the author.

1. Jonathan Griffin, text for Mary Mary, Liste 18, Basel, June 2012.
2. María Luz Cárdenas, 'A Conversation with Gego', in Nadja Rottner and Peter Weibel (eds), *Gego 1957–1988: Thinking the Line*, Hatje Cantz, Ostfildern, 2006, p.226.
3. Katharine Stout, *Contemporary Drawing from the 1960s to Now*, Tate Publishing, London, 2014, p.24.
4. Paul Klee, *Creative Confession and Other Writings*, Tate Publishing, London, 2014.
5. From the 1930s onwards, as ill health prevented Matisse from painting, he began to cut into painted paper with scissors to make drafts for a number of commissions. Over time and until his death at the age of 85 in 1954, Matisse chose cut-outs over painting: he had invented a new medium.

flowering of the rod
aluminium, steel, gouache,
water-based oil paint, chain

Aquaria
aluminium sheet, steel, canvas,
watercolour, oil paint, pastel,
filler, rivets

walls and clouds backing the view
steel and brass rod, aluminium
sheet, oil paint, aluminium paint,
metal filler

Draft overlapped
steel rod, brass rod,
aluminium sheet, oil paint, canvas,
metal filler, glass

Universal arrangement and
Staging
steel rod, steel flat bar, aluminium sheet, gouache, acrylic paint, metal filler, mirror and steel base

Love letter
aluminium sheet, steel rod, steel bar, canvas, oil paint, watercolour, acrylic paint, aquarelle, metal filler on steel and mirror plinth

Adolescent
steel rod, brass rod, aluminium sheet, canvas, oil paint, acrylic paint, metal filler

Seascape proposal
steel rod, aluminium sheet, acrylic paint, gouache, metal filler

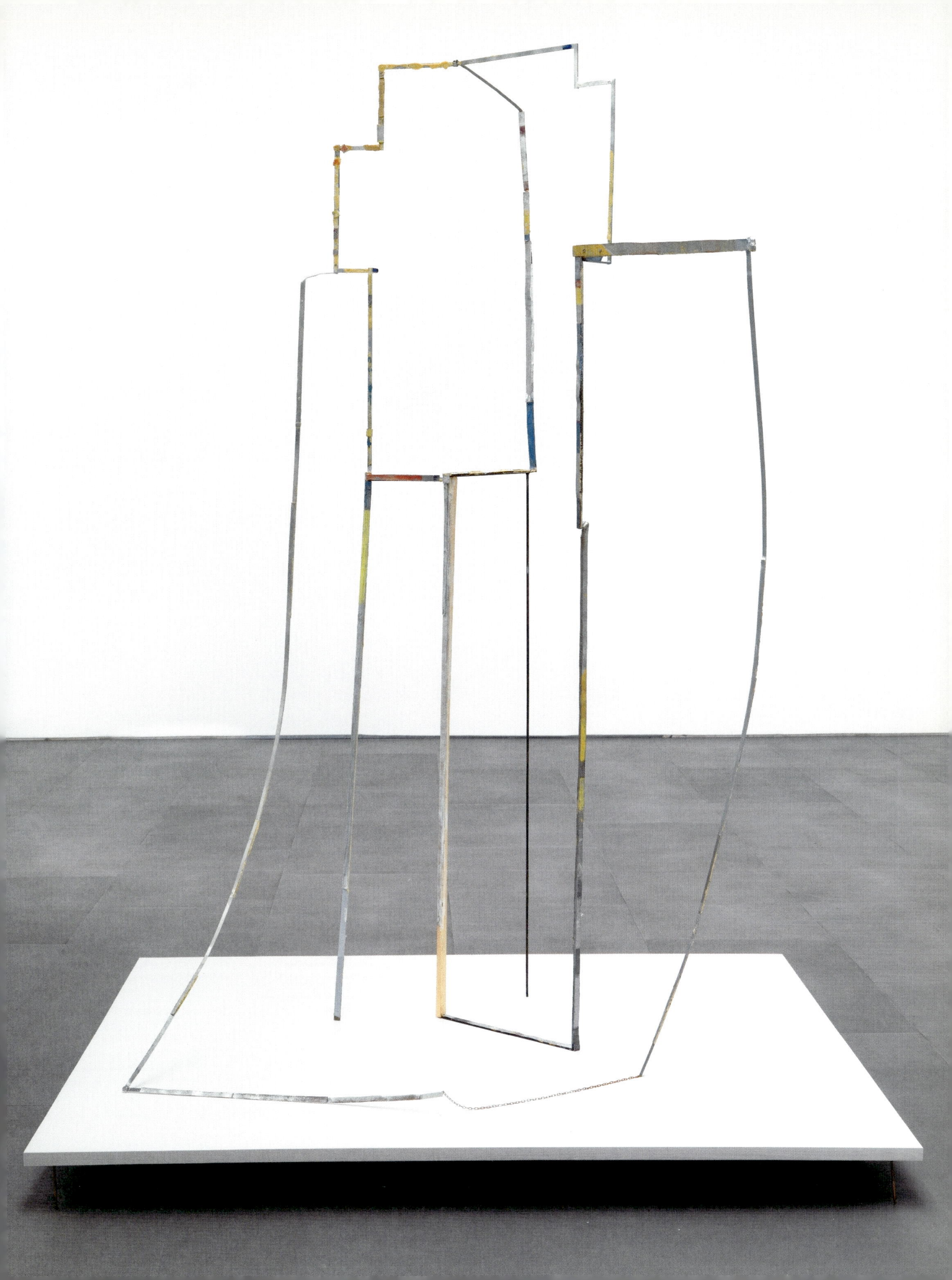

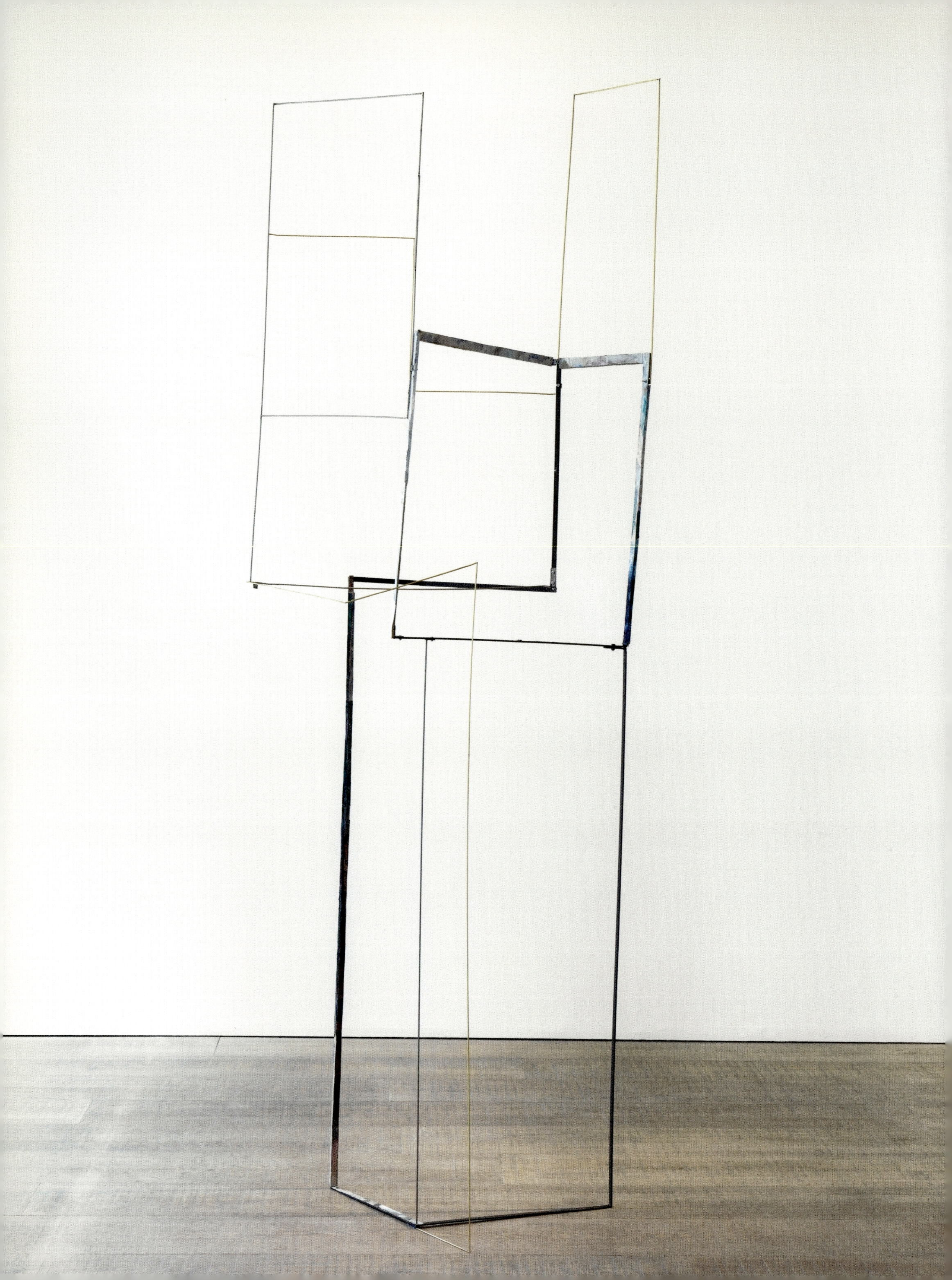

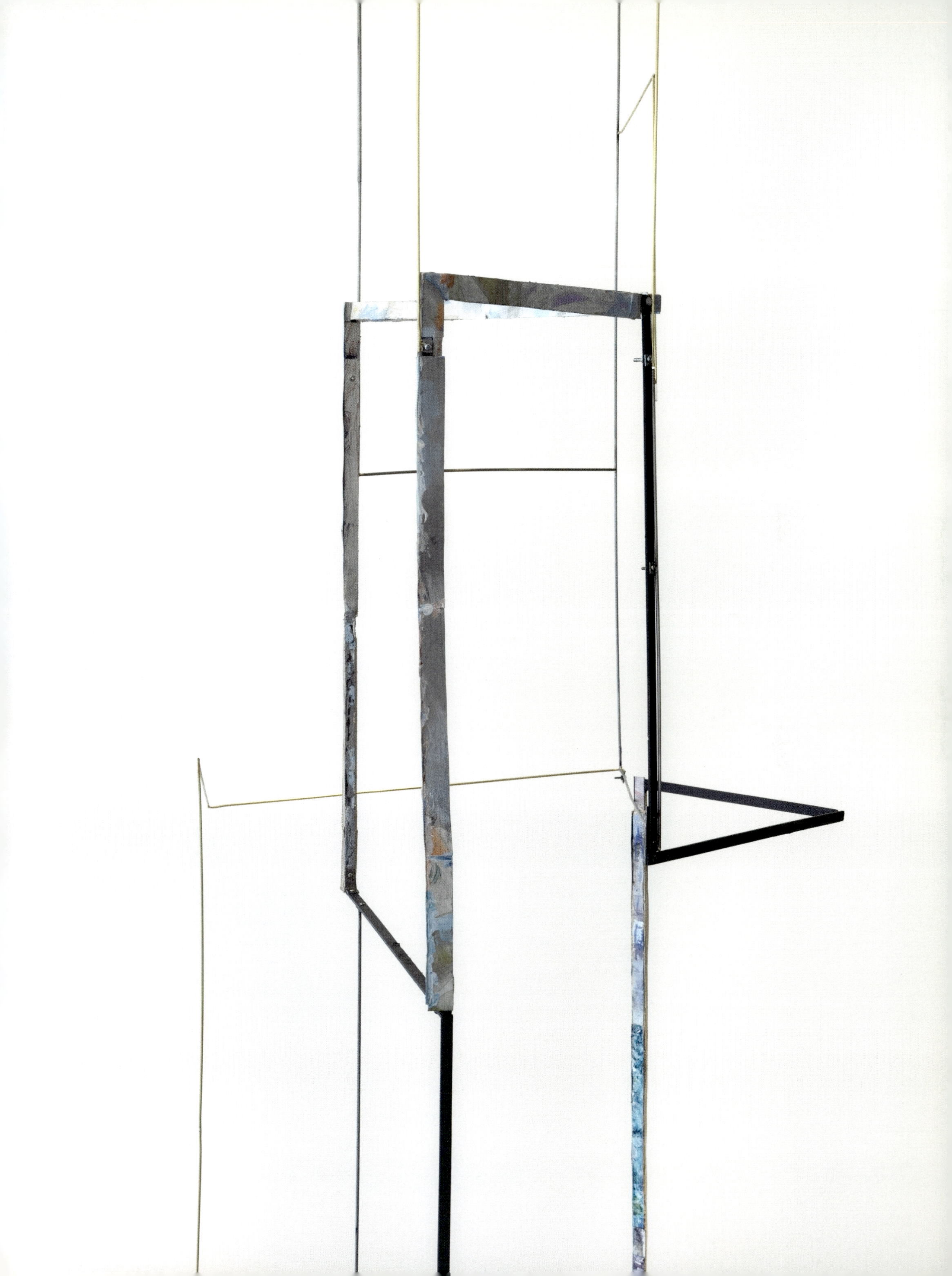

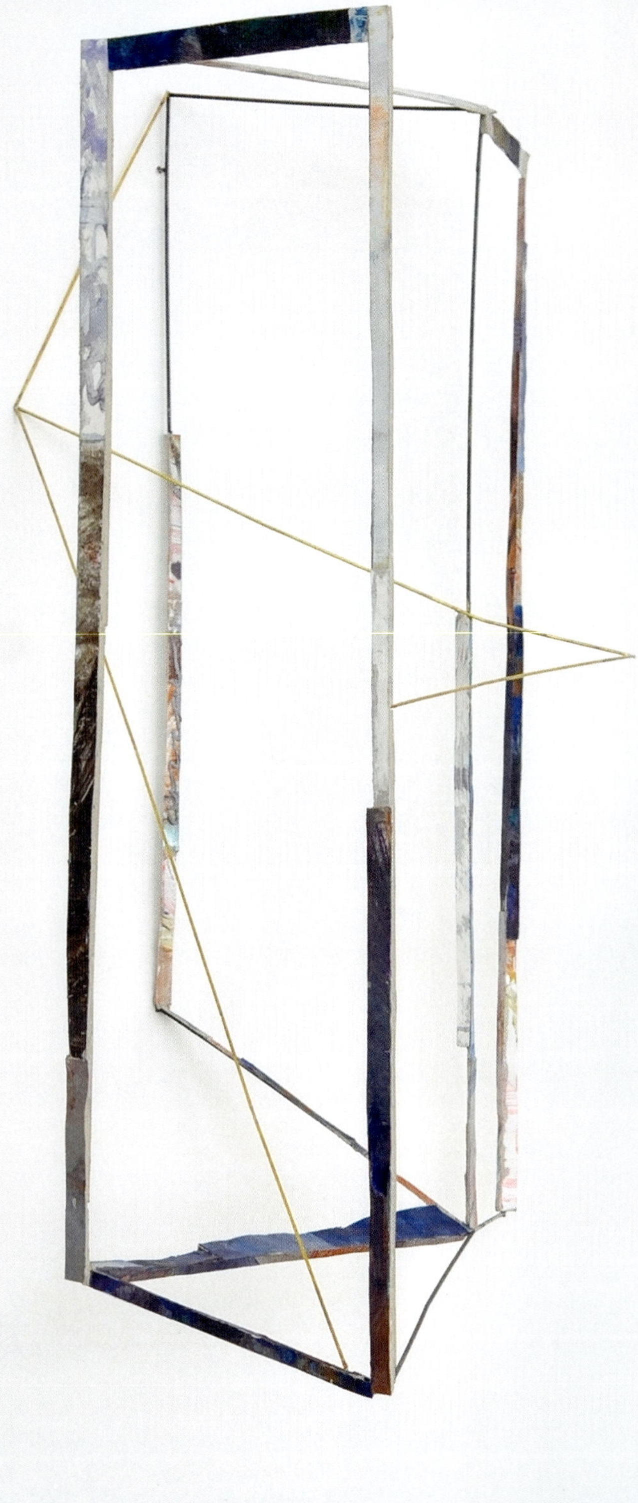

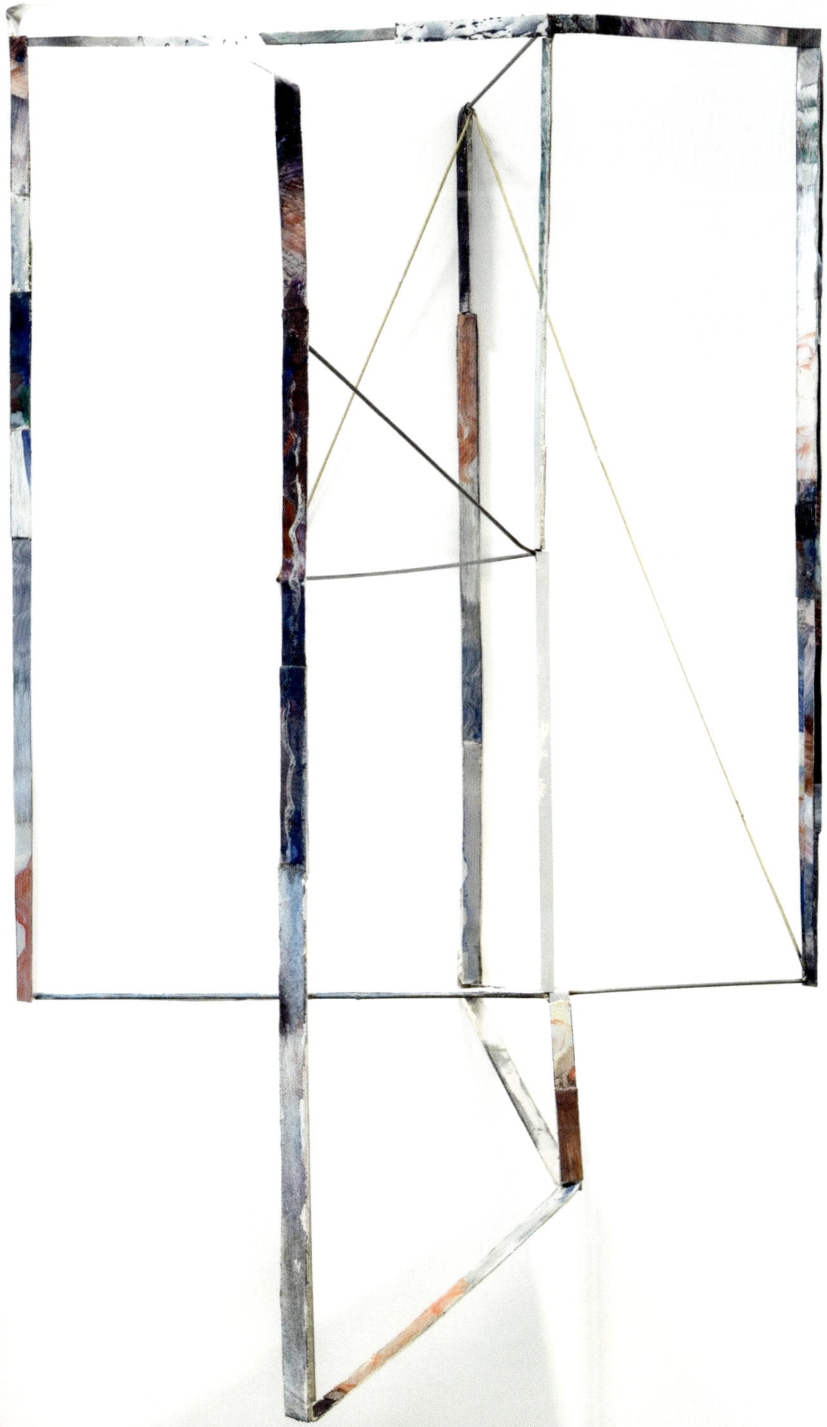

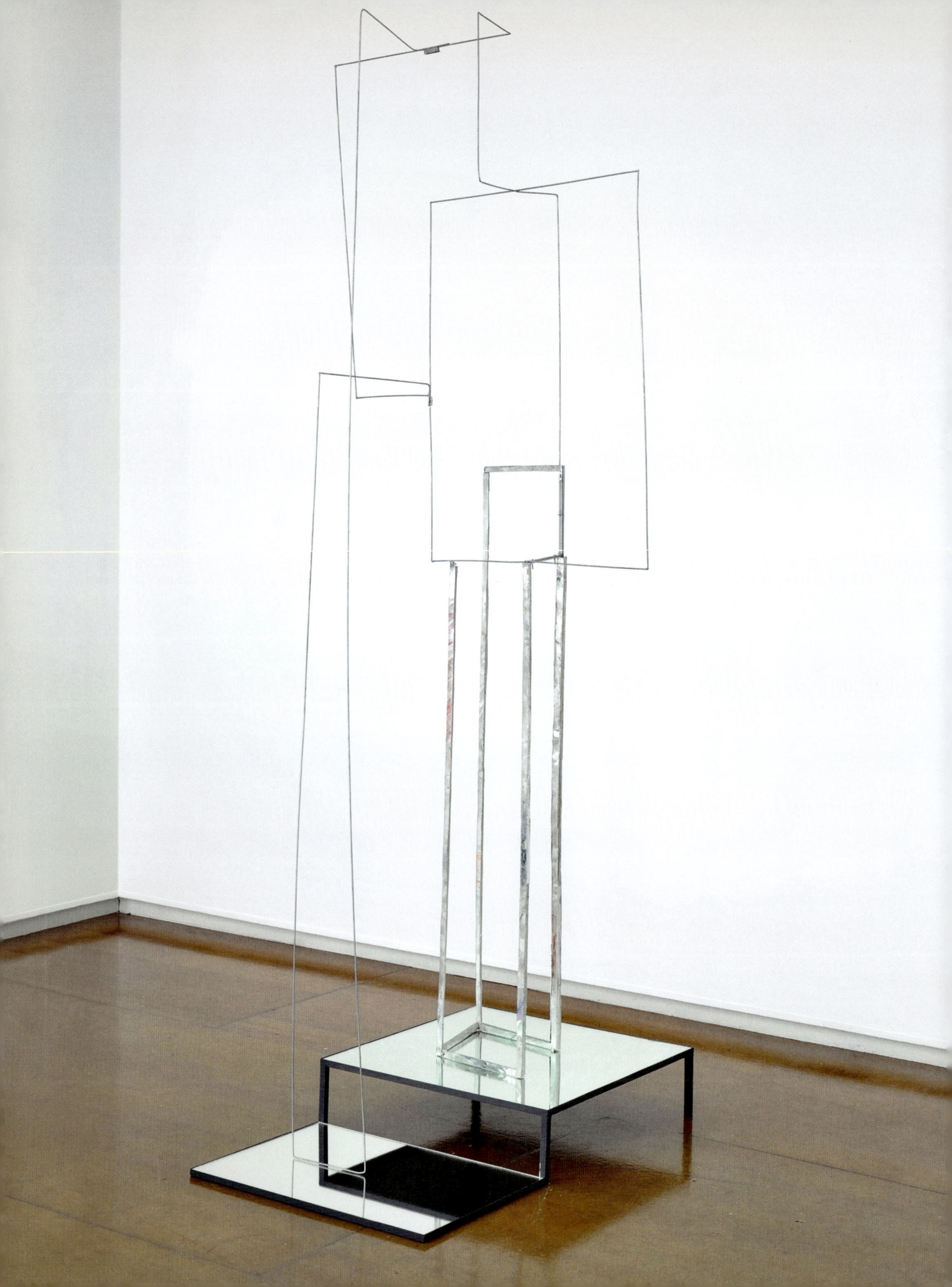

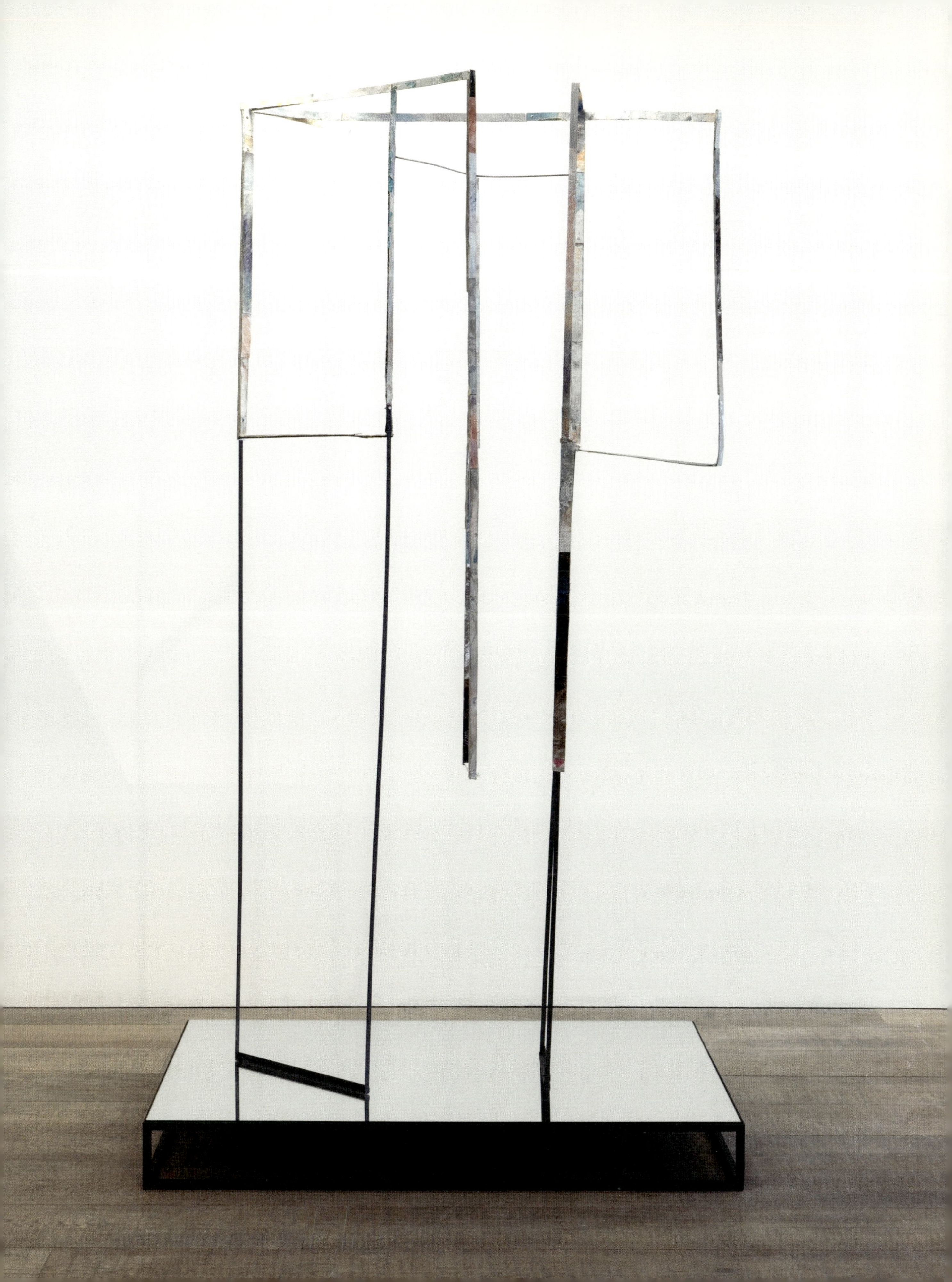

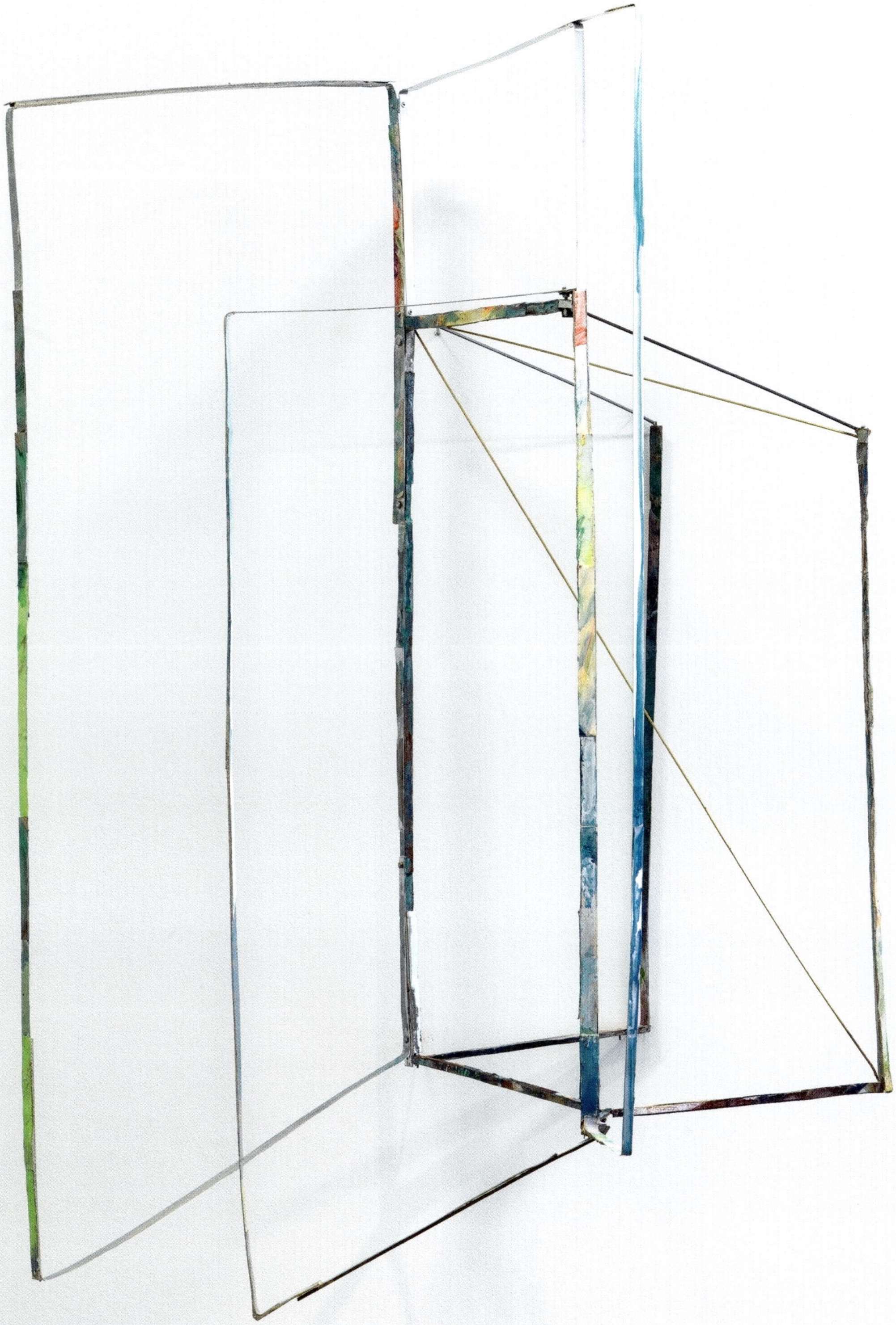

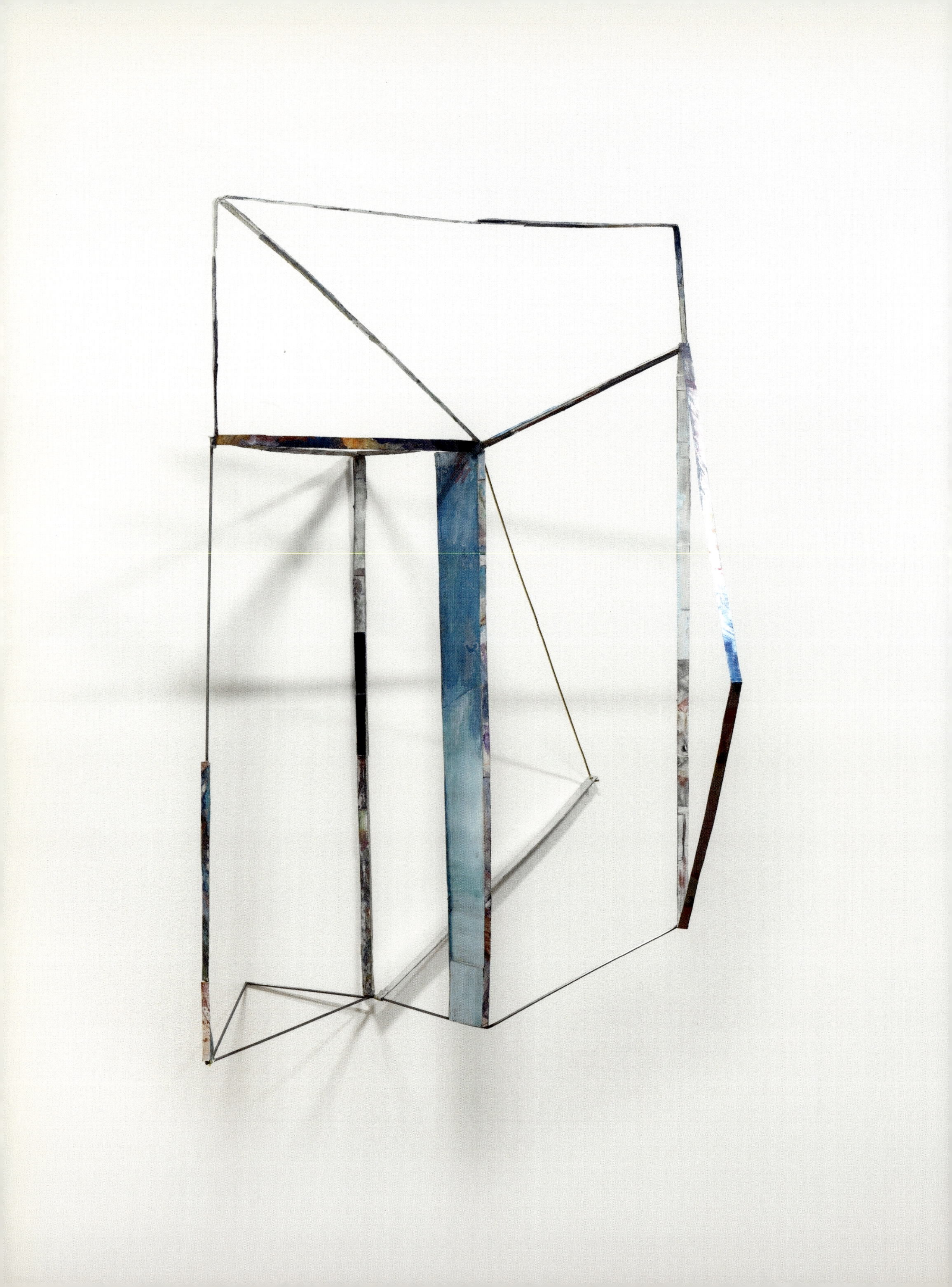

Composition with furling symphonia
brass and steel rod, aluminium
sheet, gold powder, aluminium
powder, watercolour, gouache,
metal primer, filler

sampler
steel and brass rod, aluminium
sheet, various paints, filler

Satellite
brass and steel rod, canvas,
aluminium, various paints
and fillers

Matters
plywood, aluminium, various
paints, filler, brass rod

trawling (with triangles) – pin
brass and steel rod, aluminium
sheet, various paints, filler,
blackboard paint

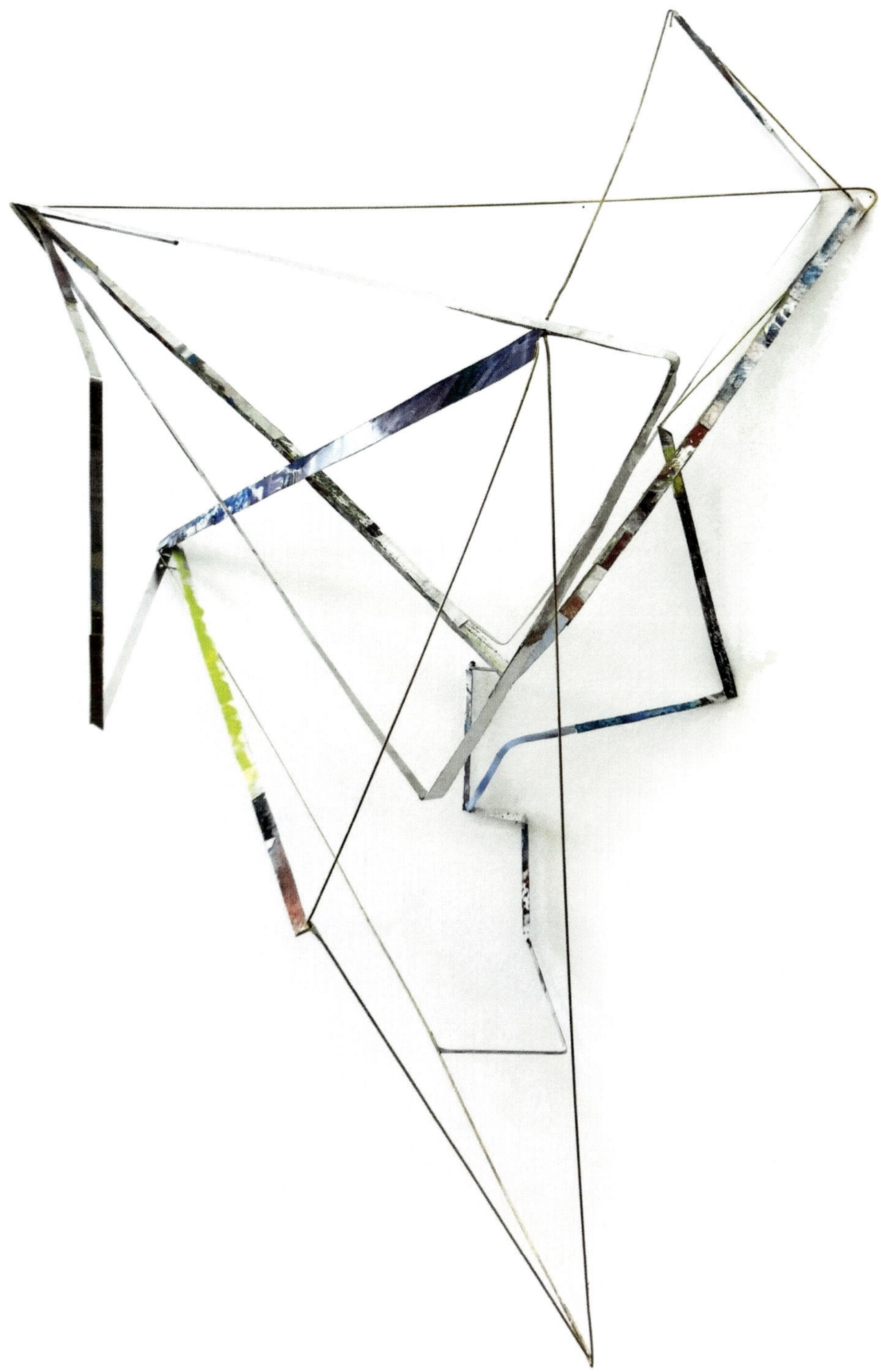

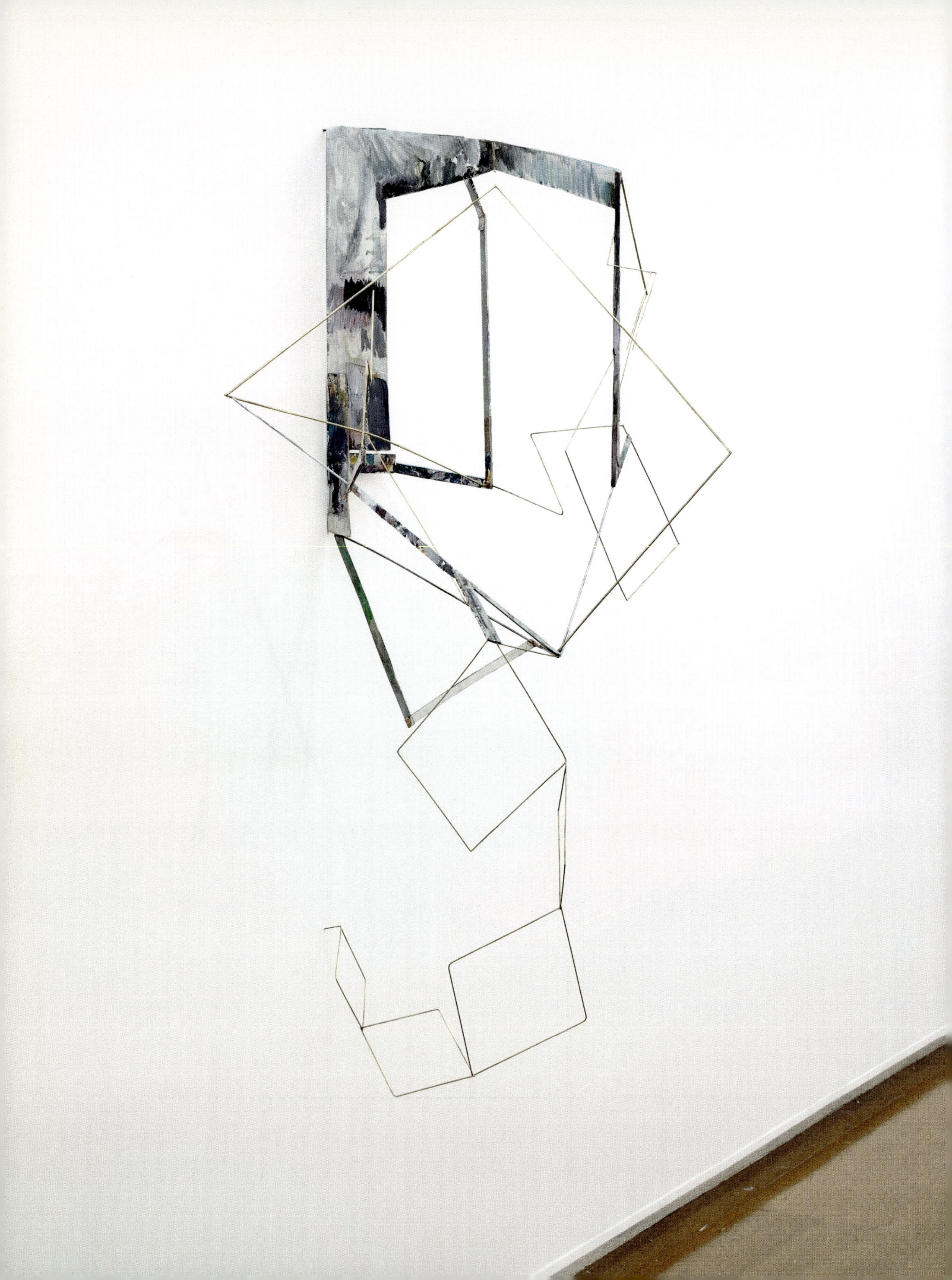

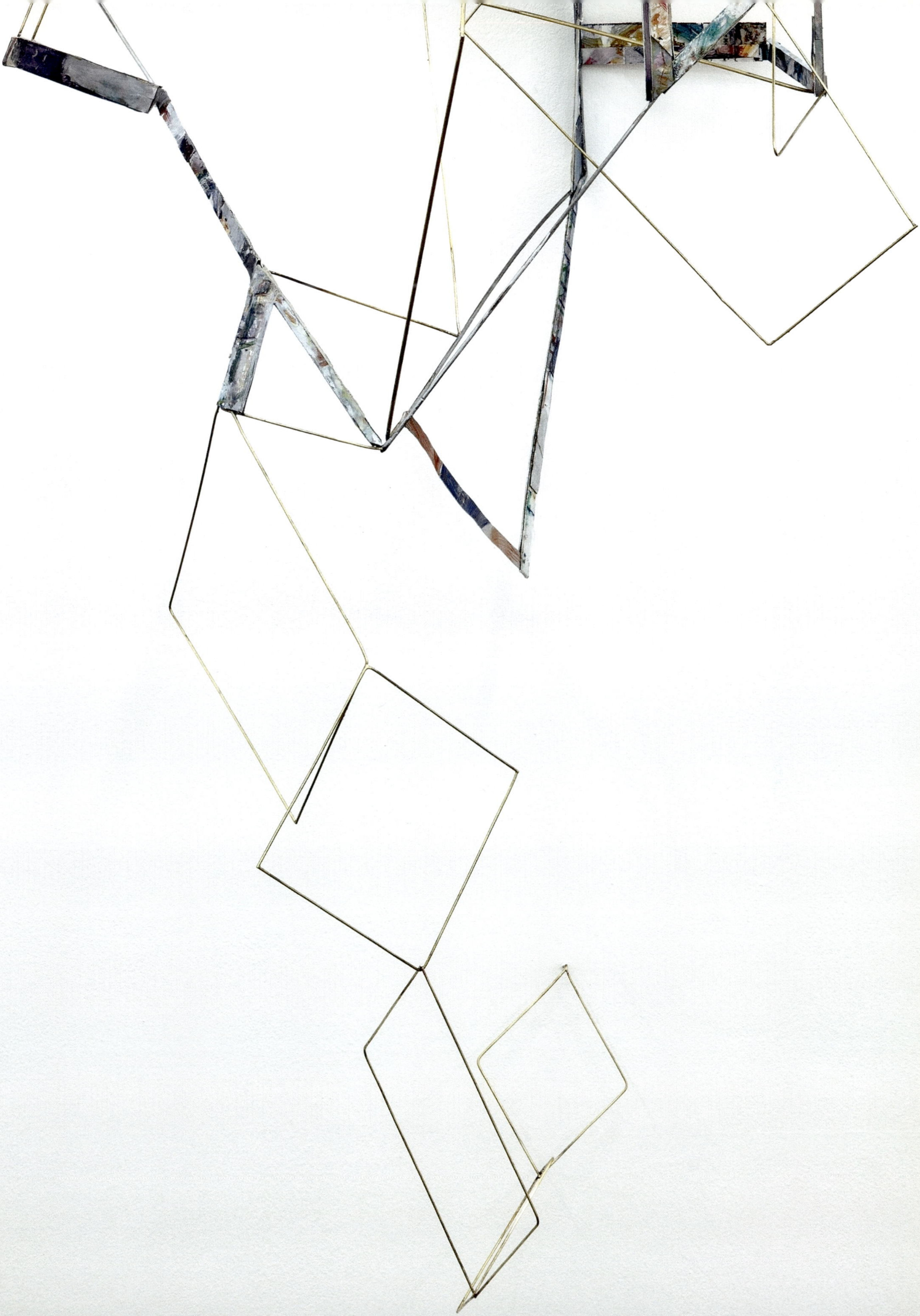

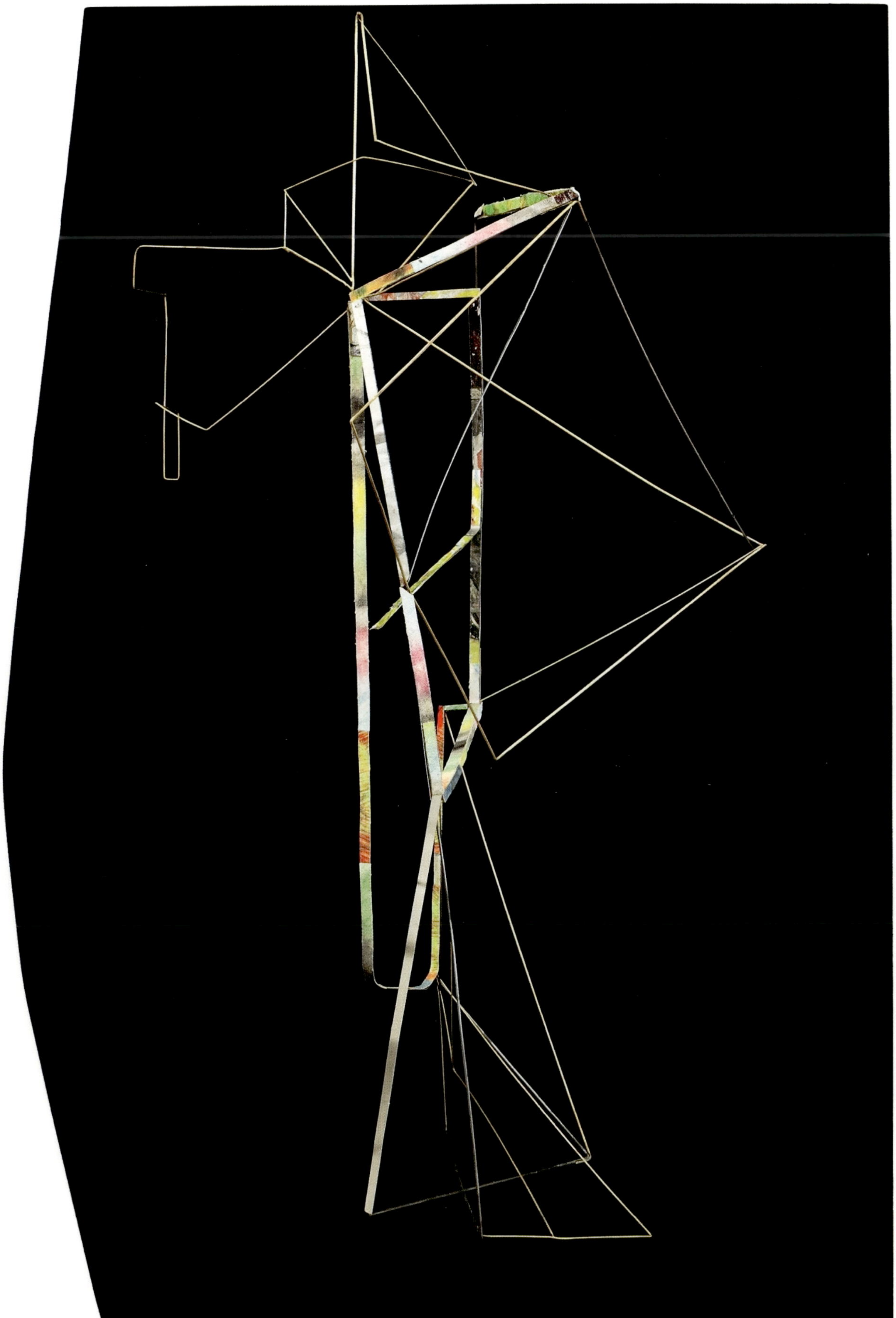

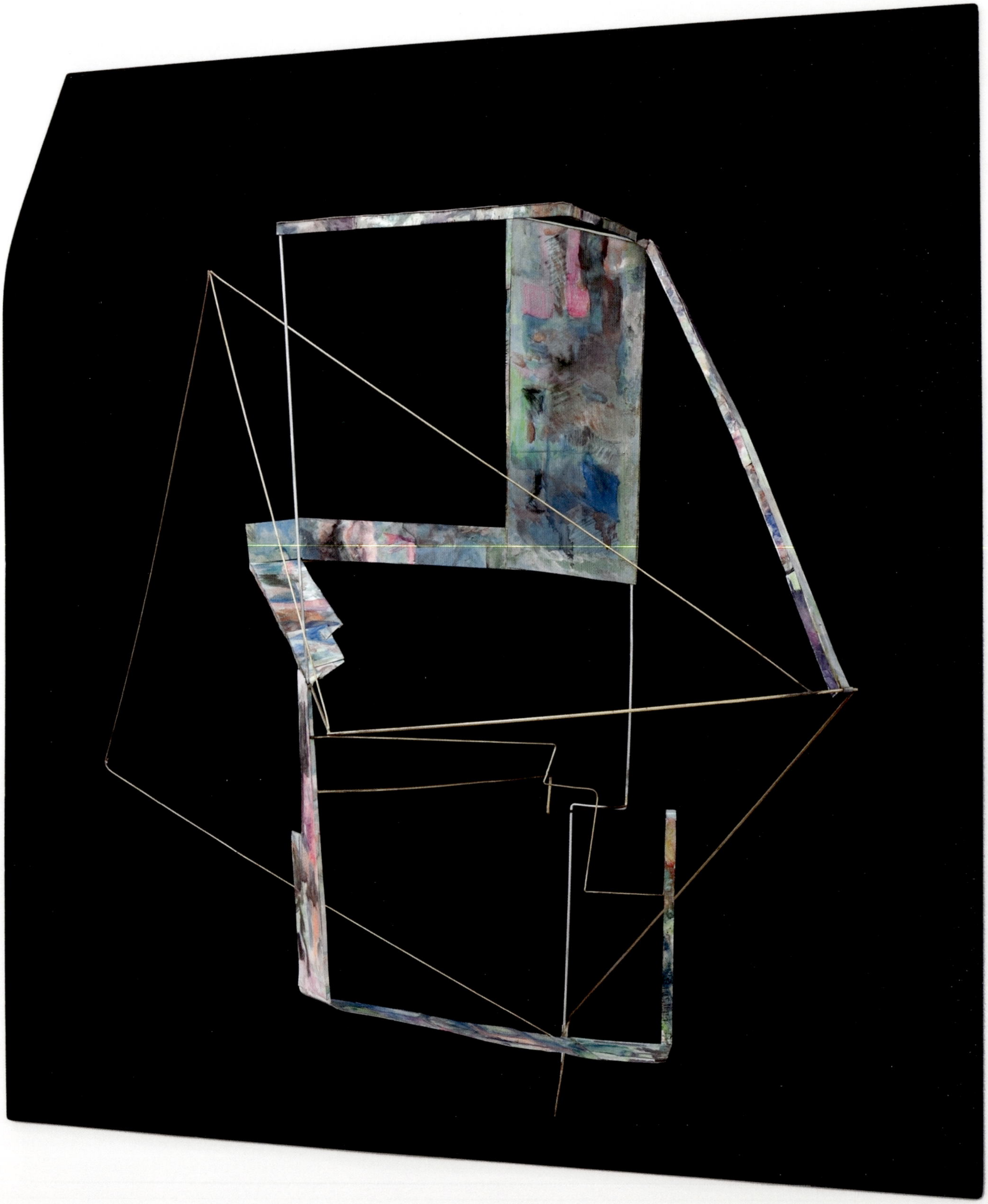

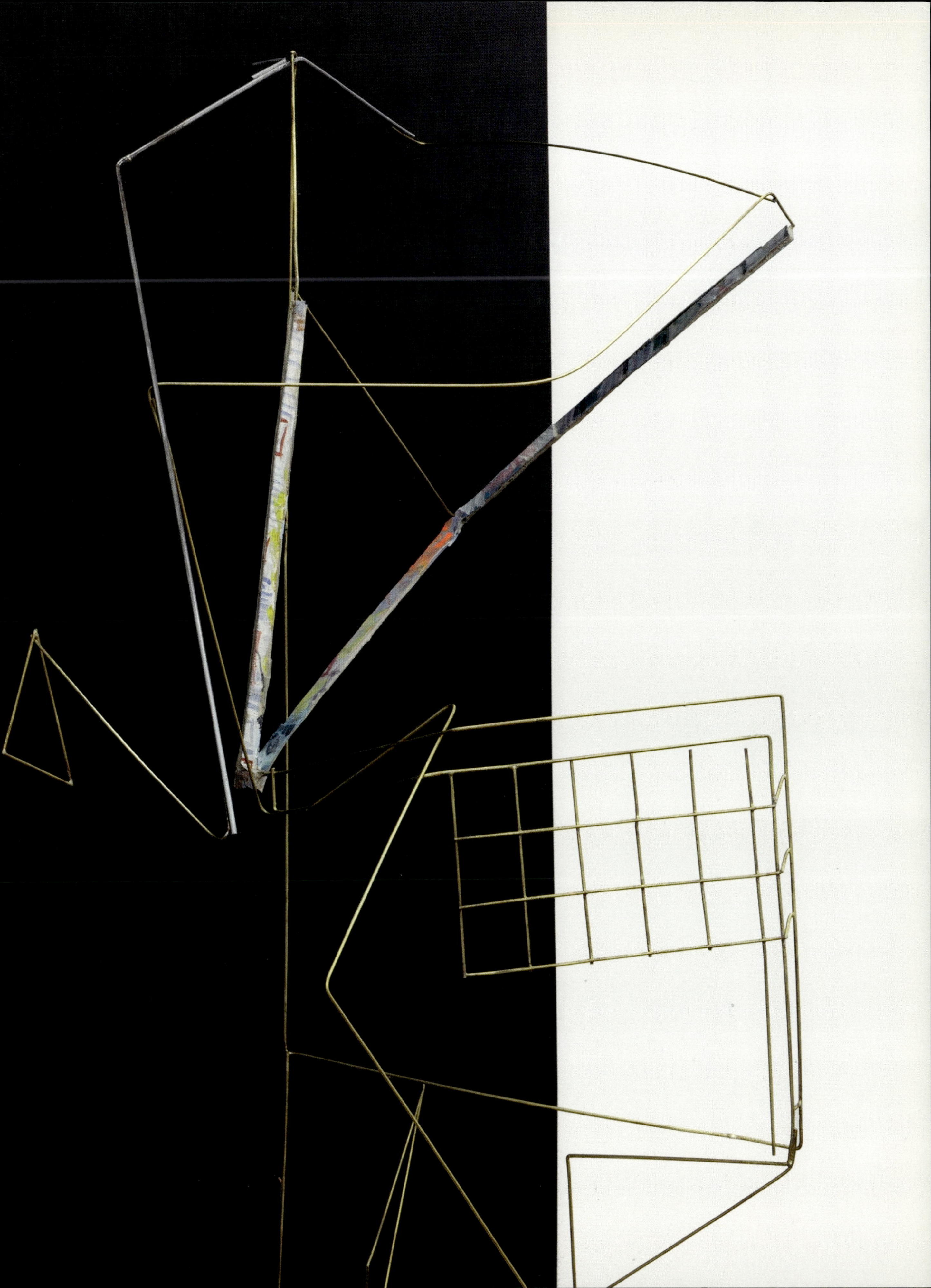

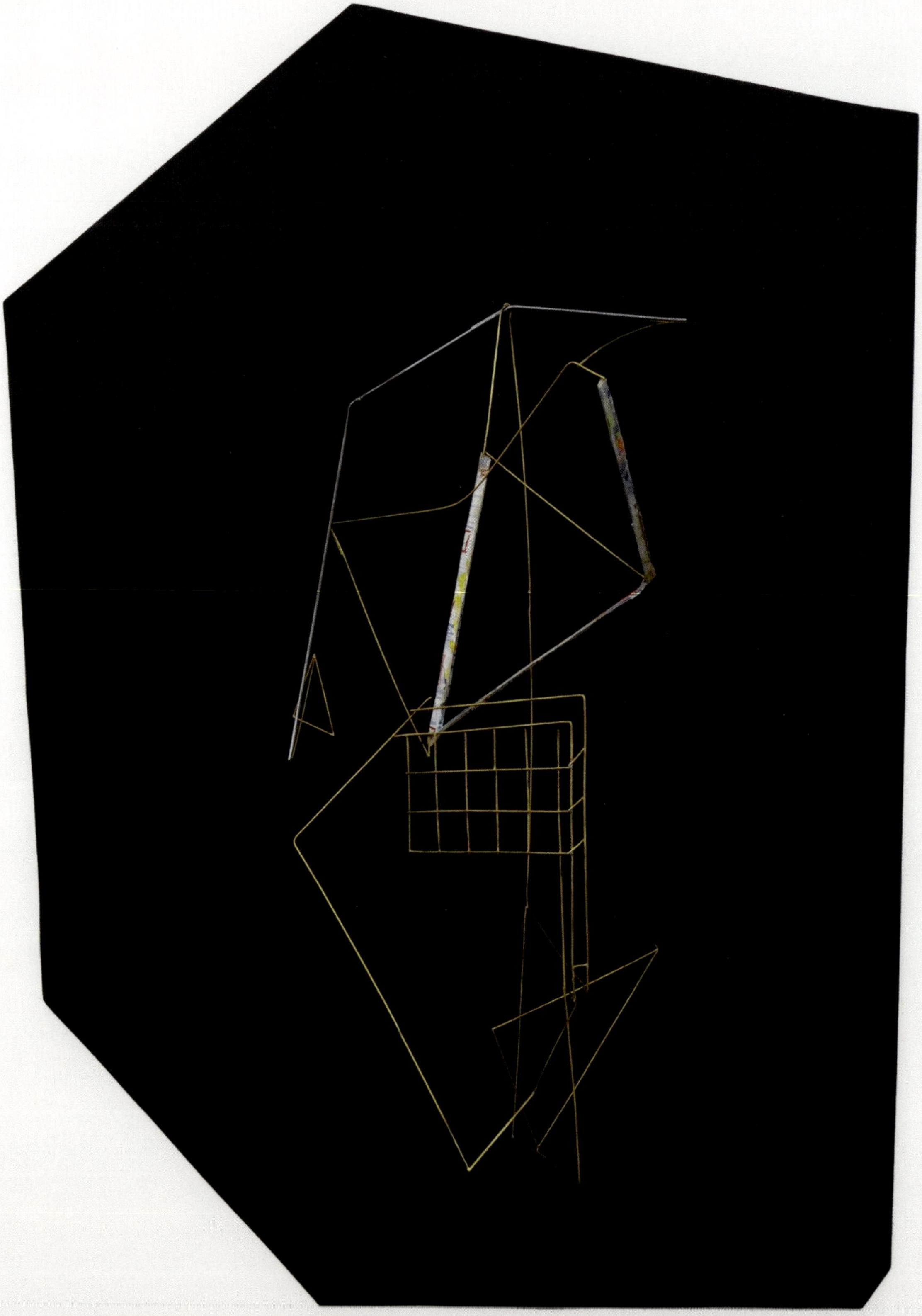

The subtle knife
brass, copper, aluminium, steel
components and fixings, plywood,
cement, various paints, glass

Patterns
glass, painted aluminium, brass,
foundation of marble chipped
whitecrete, steel fixings

Separation in the Evening
(a celestial blossom before the
yellow house)
stainless steel, stainless steel rod,
brass rod, paint

Projections of a family held
in space
brass rod, mirror polished
stainless steel panels, painted
aluminium panels, painted
aluminium plinth, bespoke
stainless steel fixings
and brackets

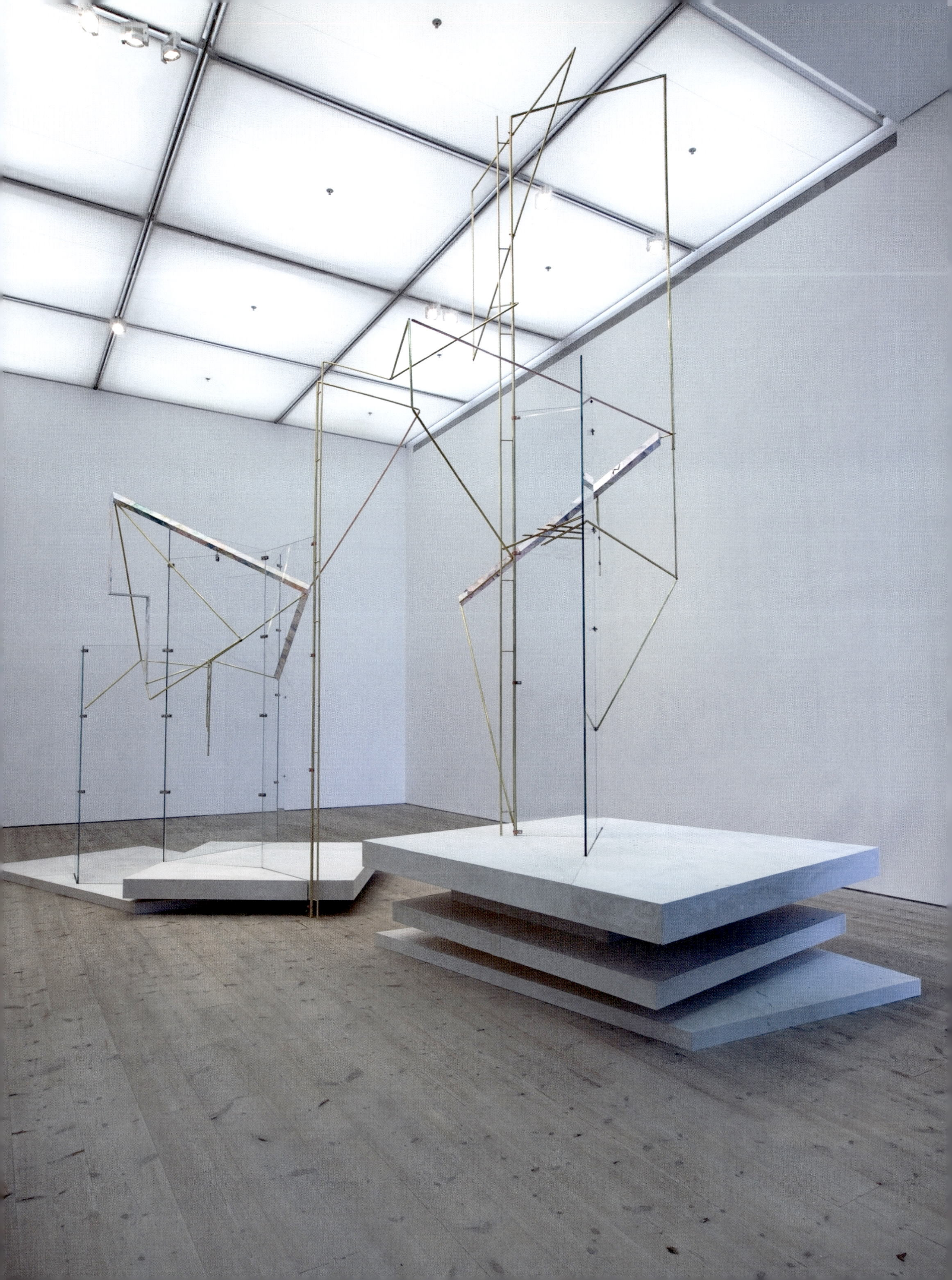

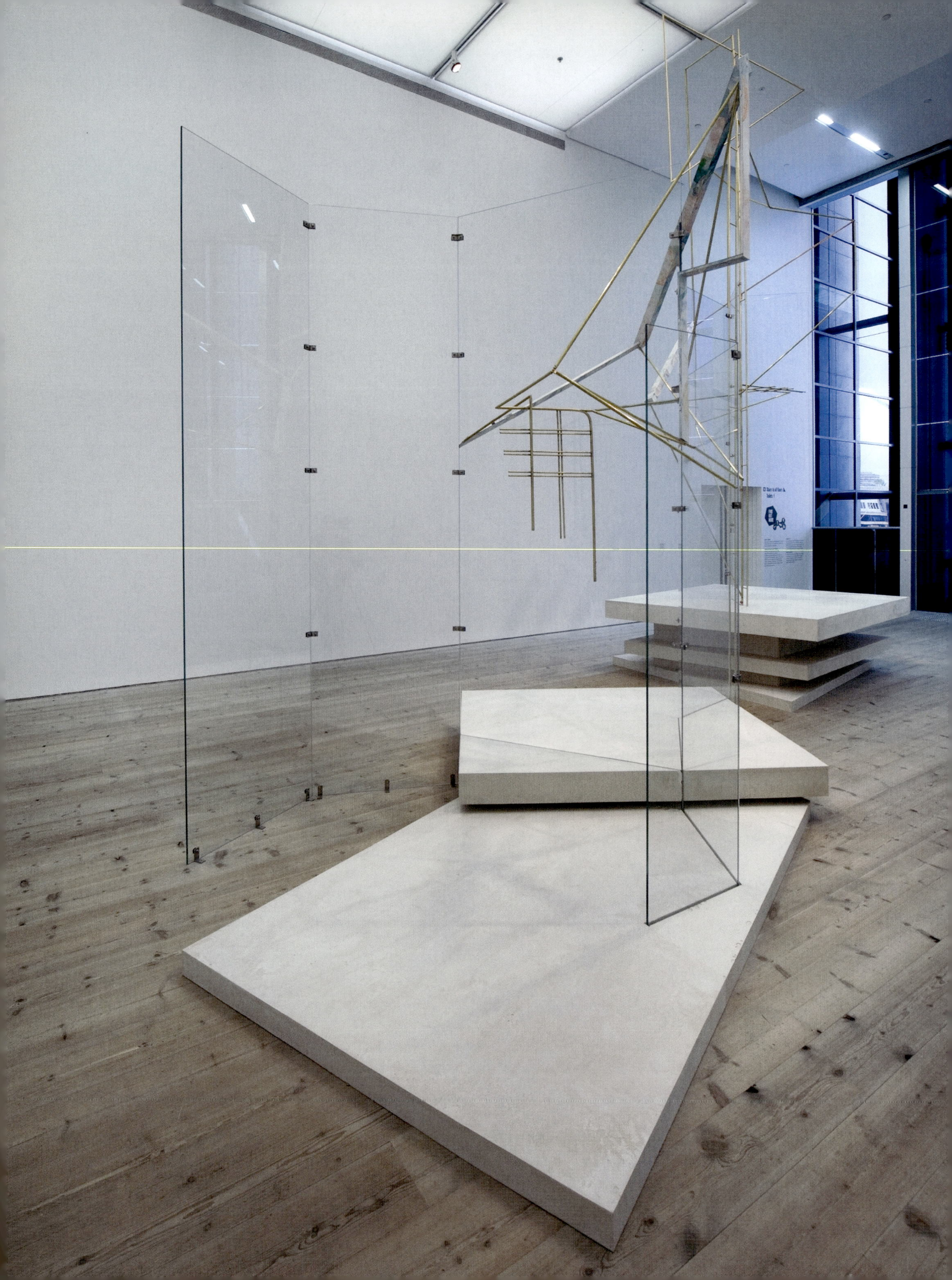

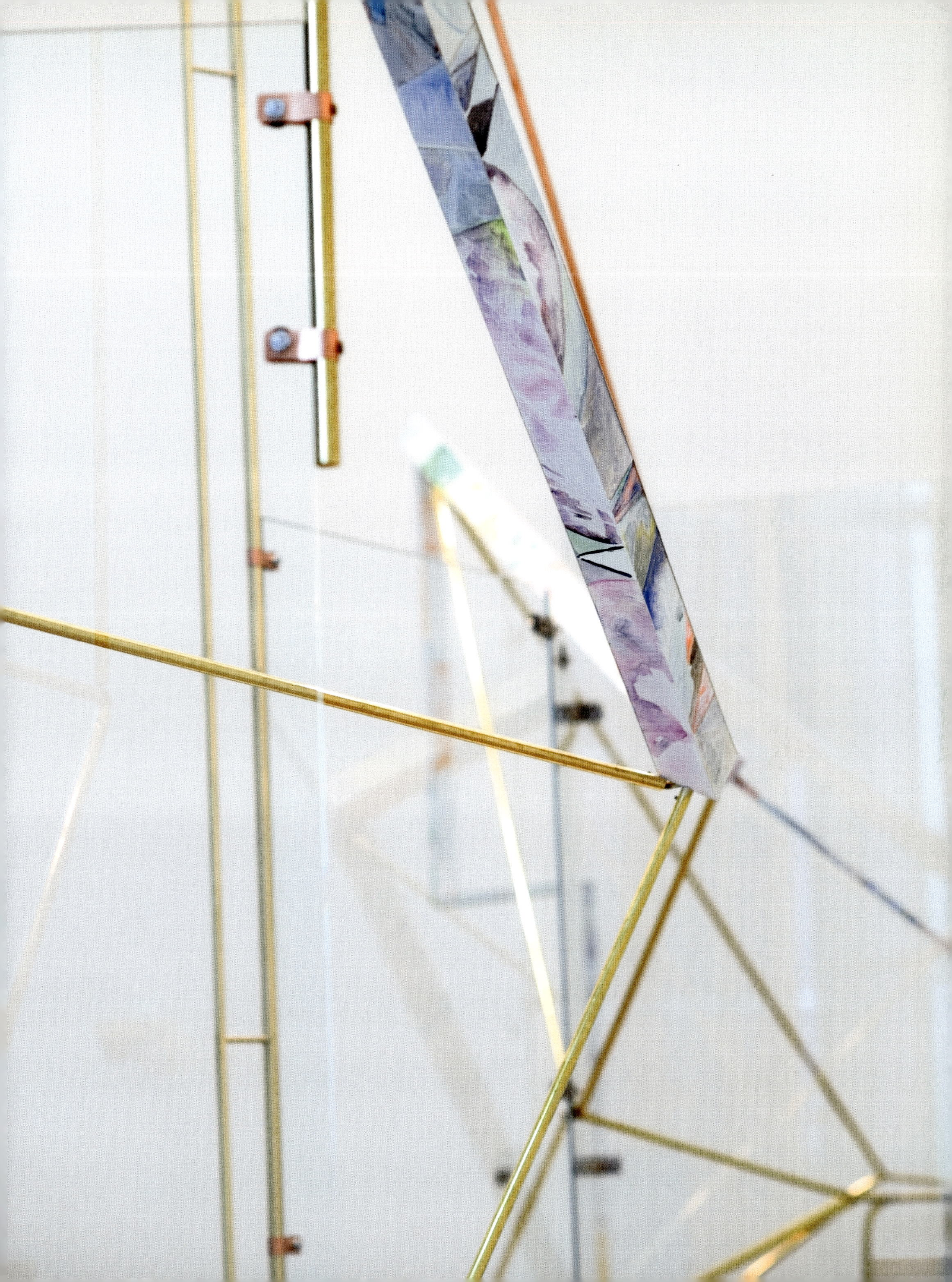

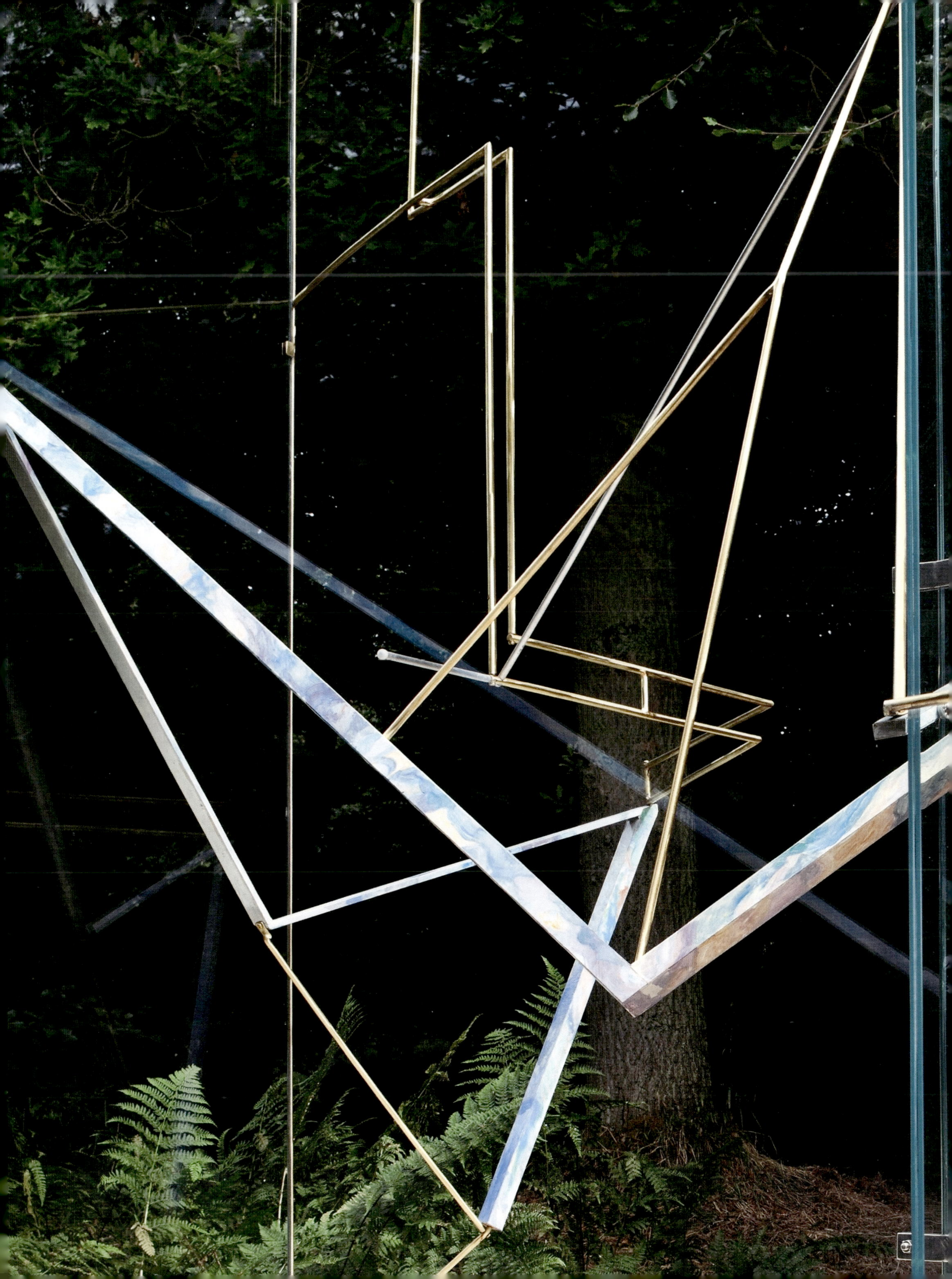

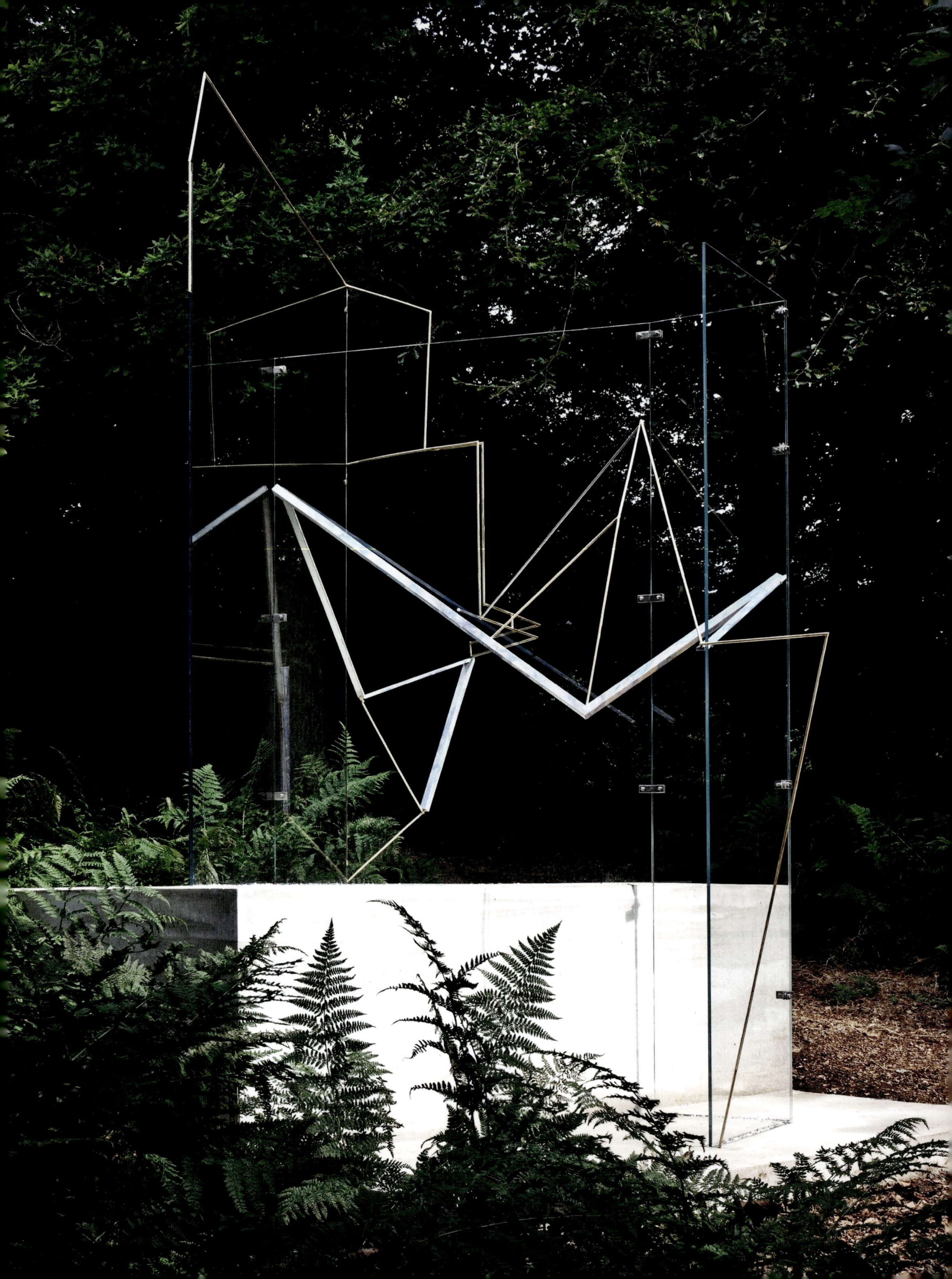

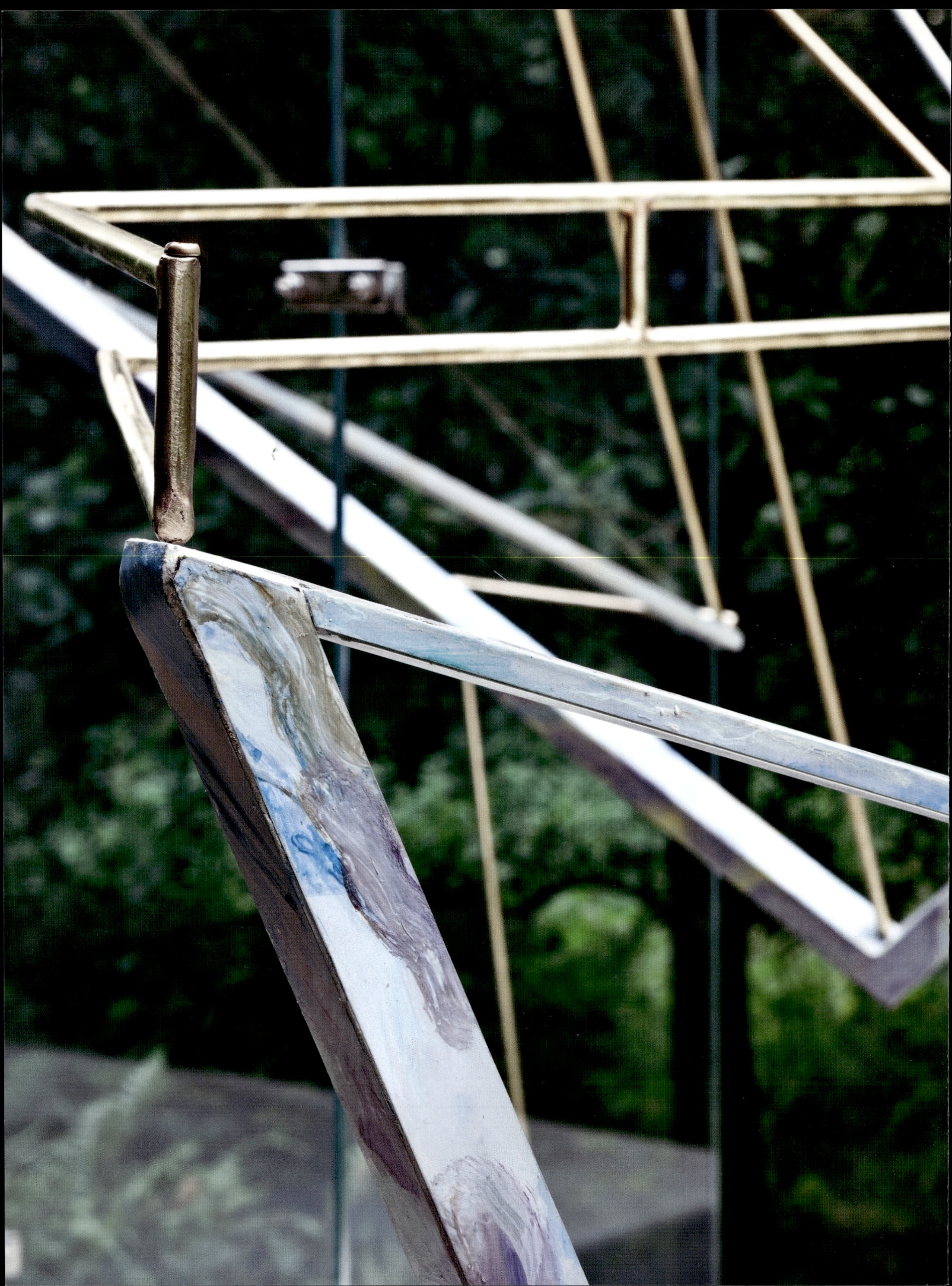

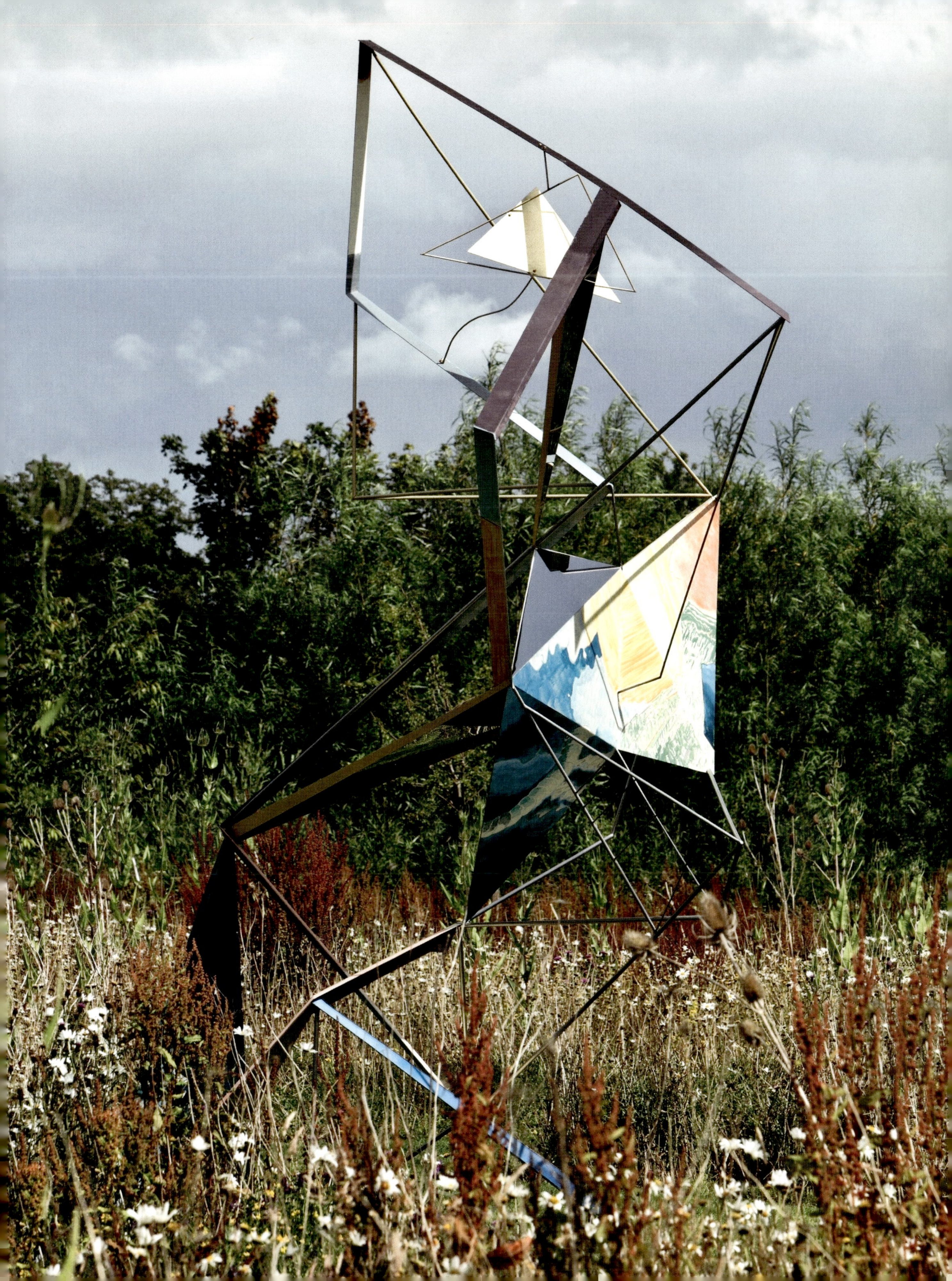

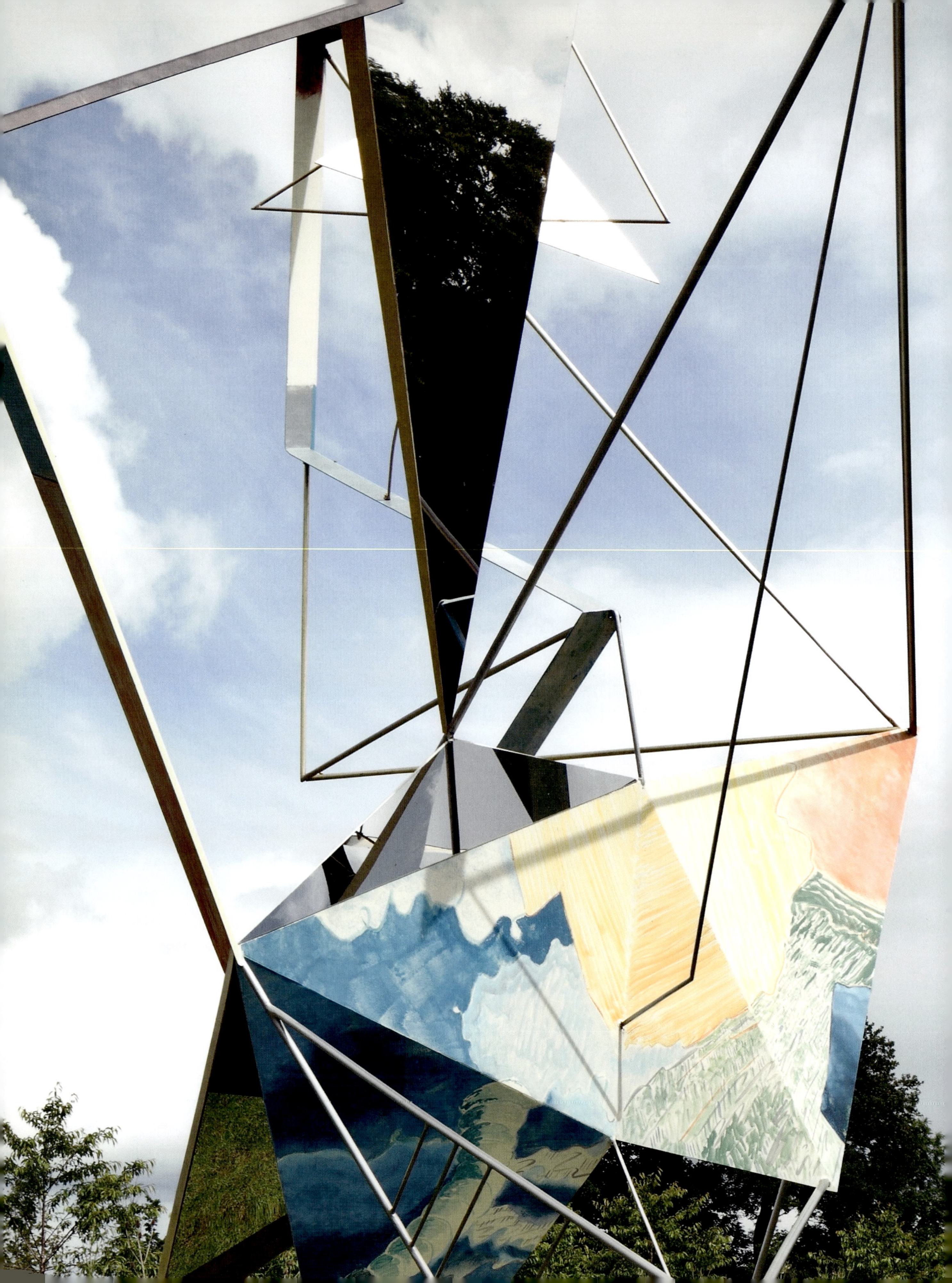

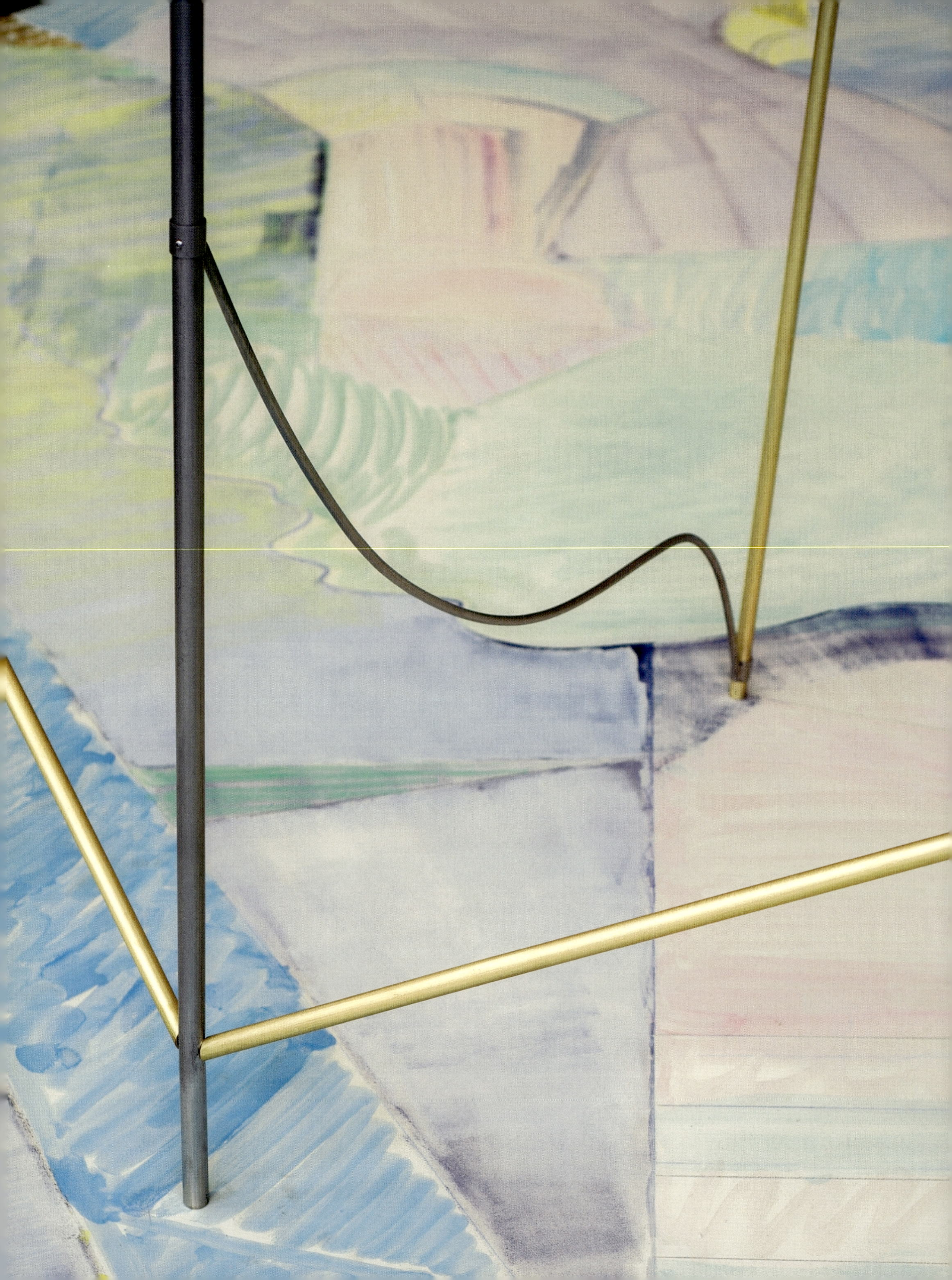

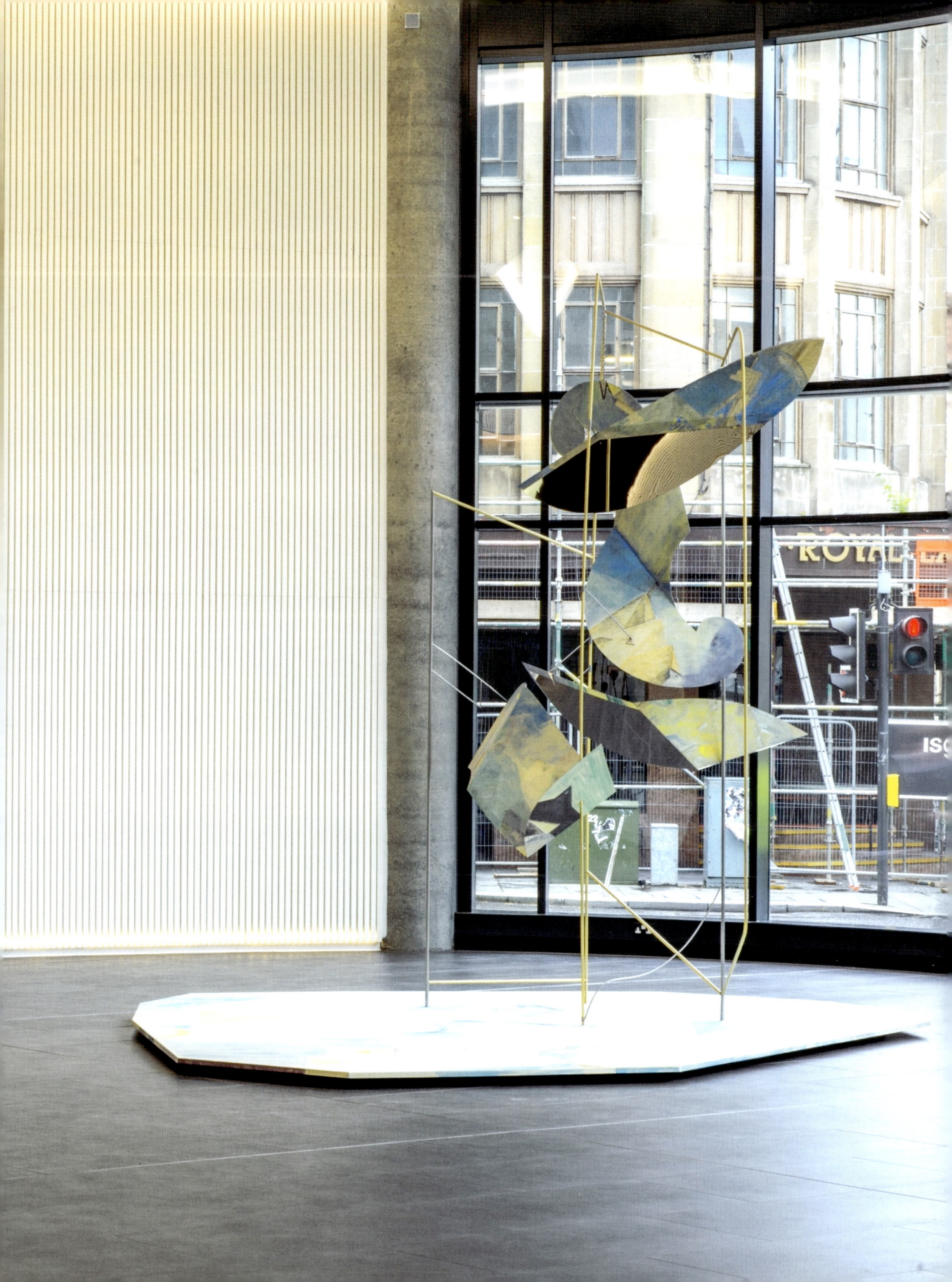
ROYAL

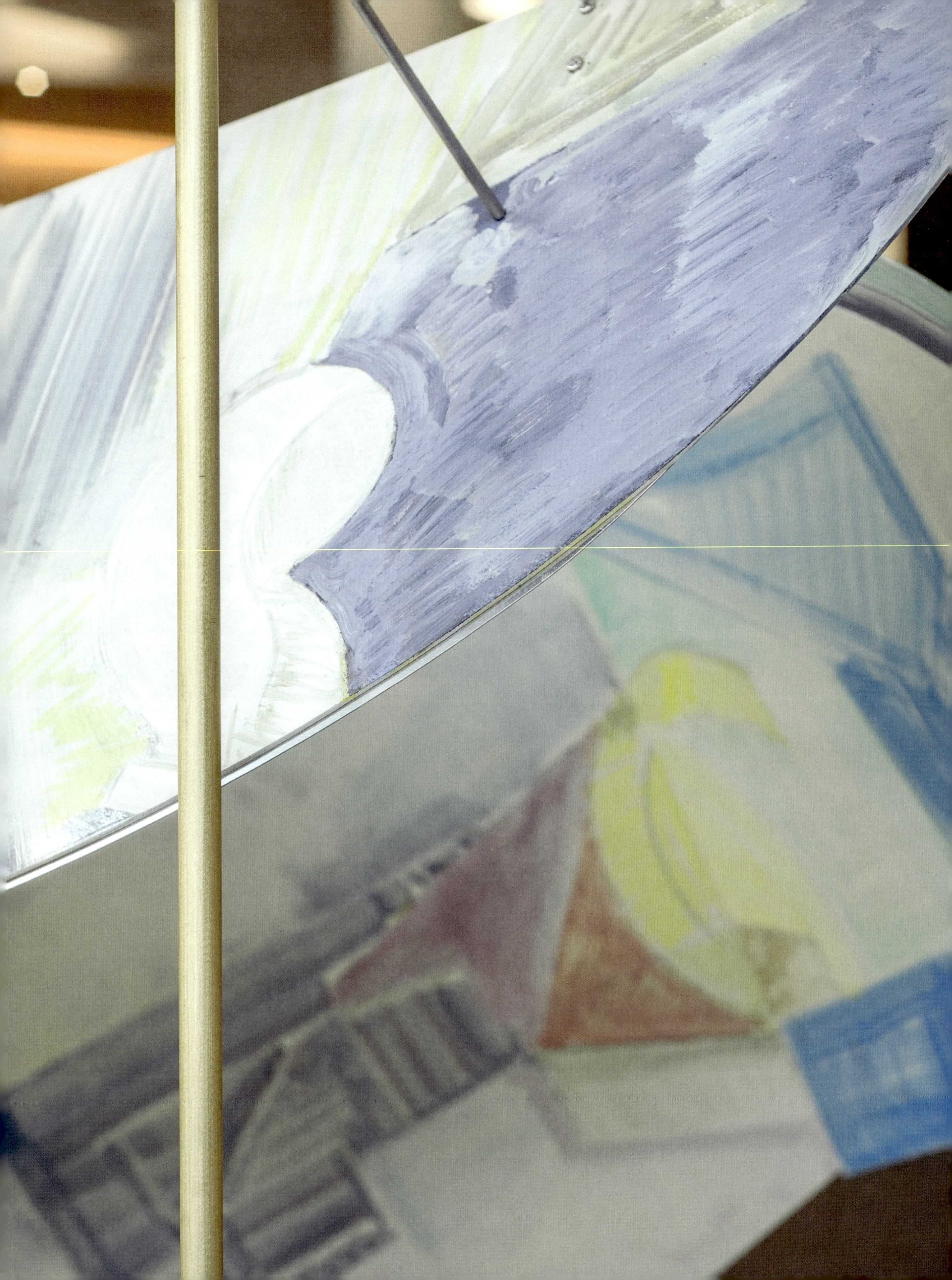

Outcast Letter
toughened glass, brass rod,
aluminium section, blackboard
paint, oil paint

Cross-sectioned feelings
toughened glass, brass and steel
rod, steel flat bar, aluminium,
blackboard paint, oil paint

In semi-darkness she reclines
and pretends to read...
toughened glass, brass rod,
steel flat bar, aluminium section,
blackboard paint, oil paint

loopholes of self expression
aluminium sheet, brass and steel
rod, steel, oil paint, blackboard
paint, chalk

HOURS BECOME HANDS (Foliage of Palms)
aluminium sheet, brass and steel rod, various paints, brass fixings

The Human Family
aluminium sheet, brass and steel rod, various paints, brass fixings

cut up dream and fold in time/order/space
aluminium sheet, brass and steel rod, oil paint, blackboard paint, chalk

Vase painting from a cylix: discussing a picture
aluminium sheet, brass and steel rod, oil paint, blackboard paint, steel, chalk

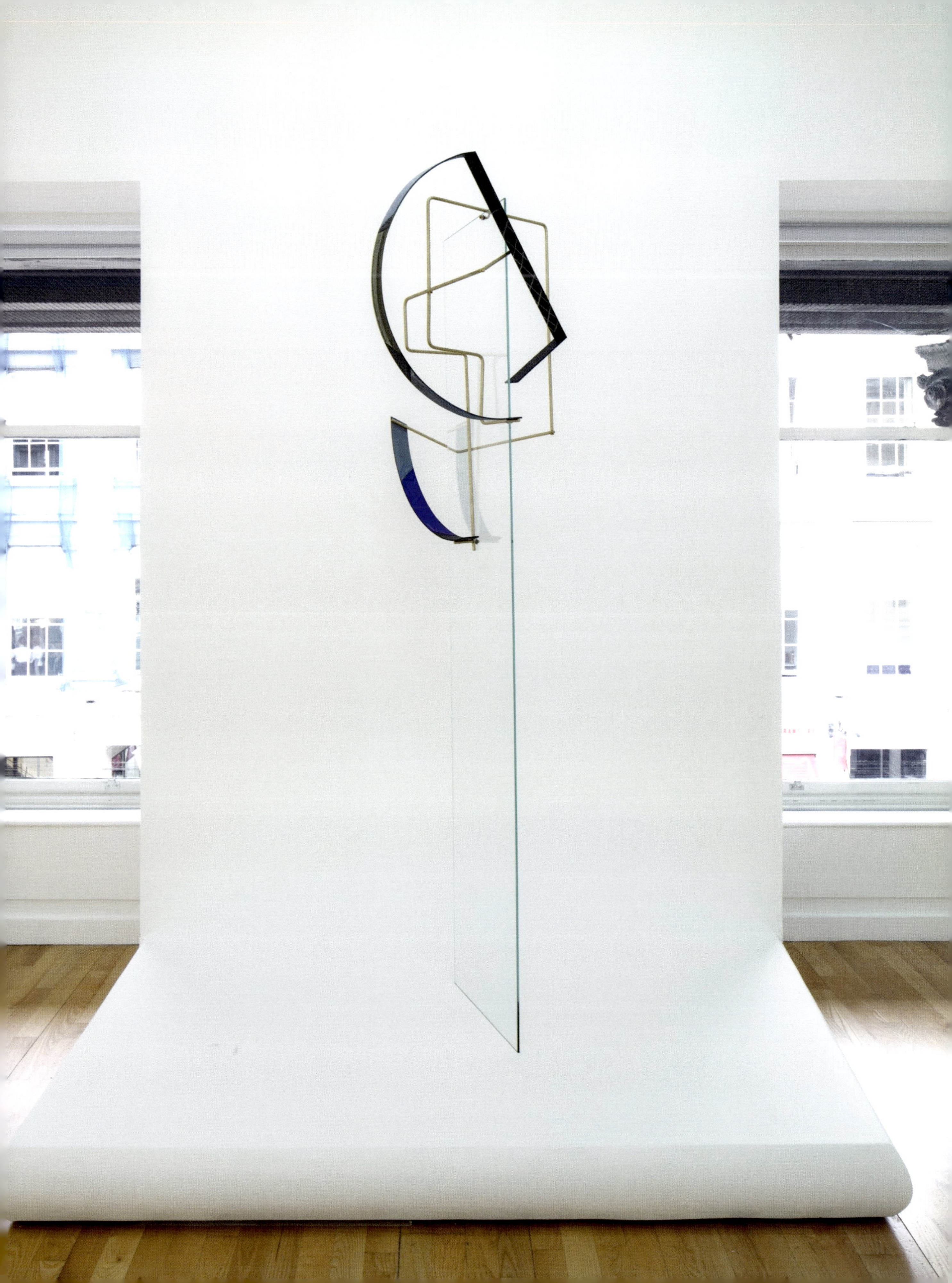

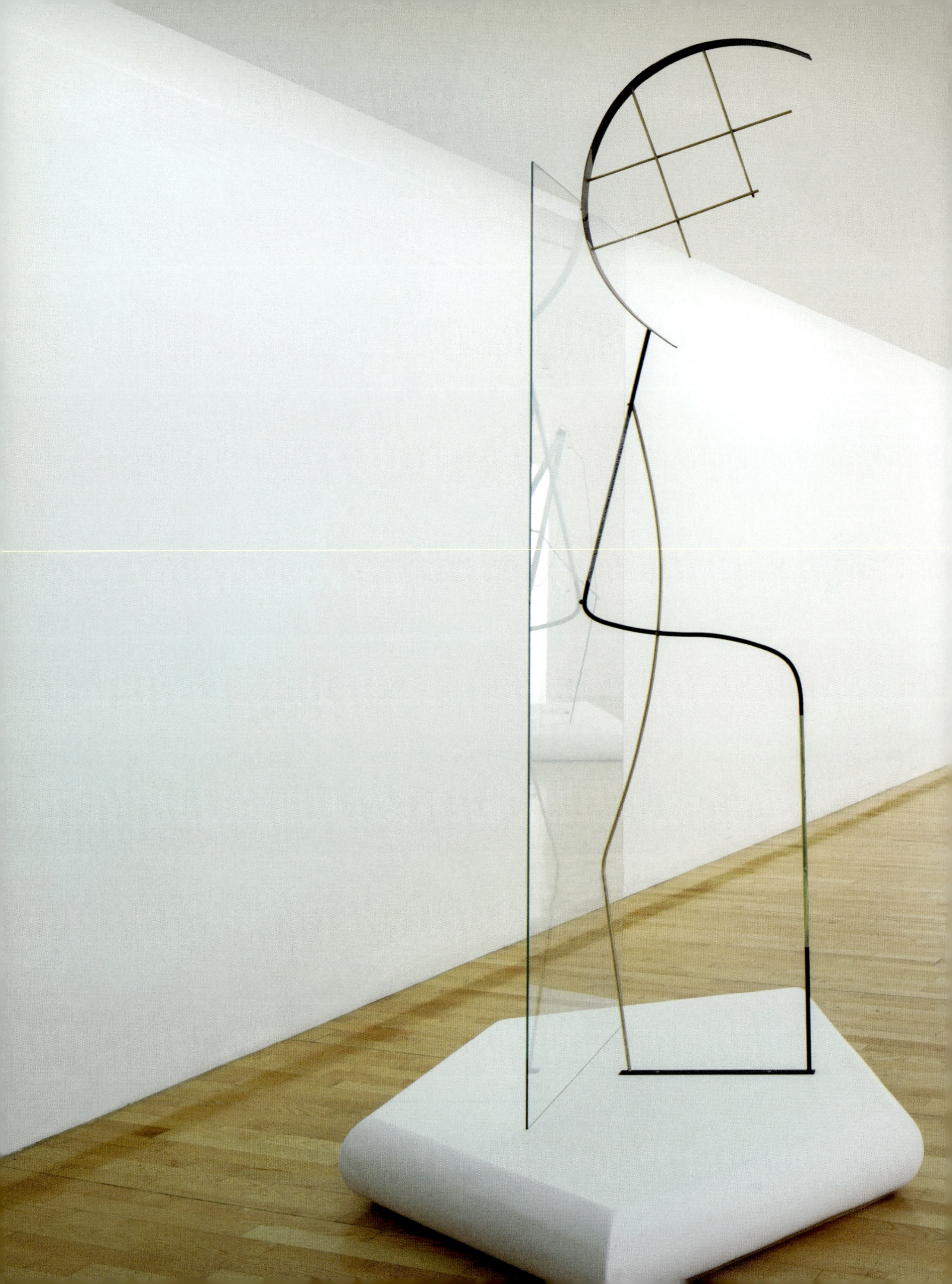

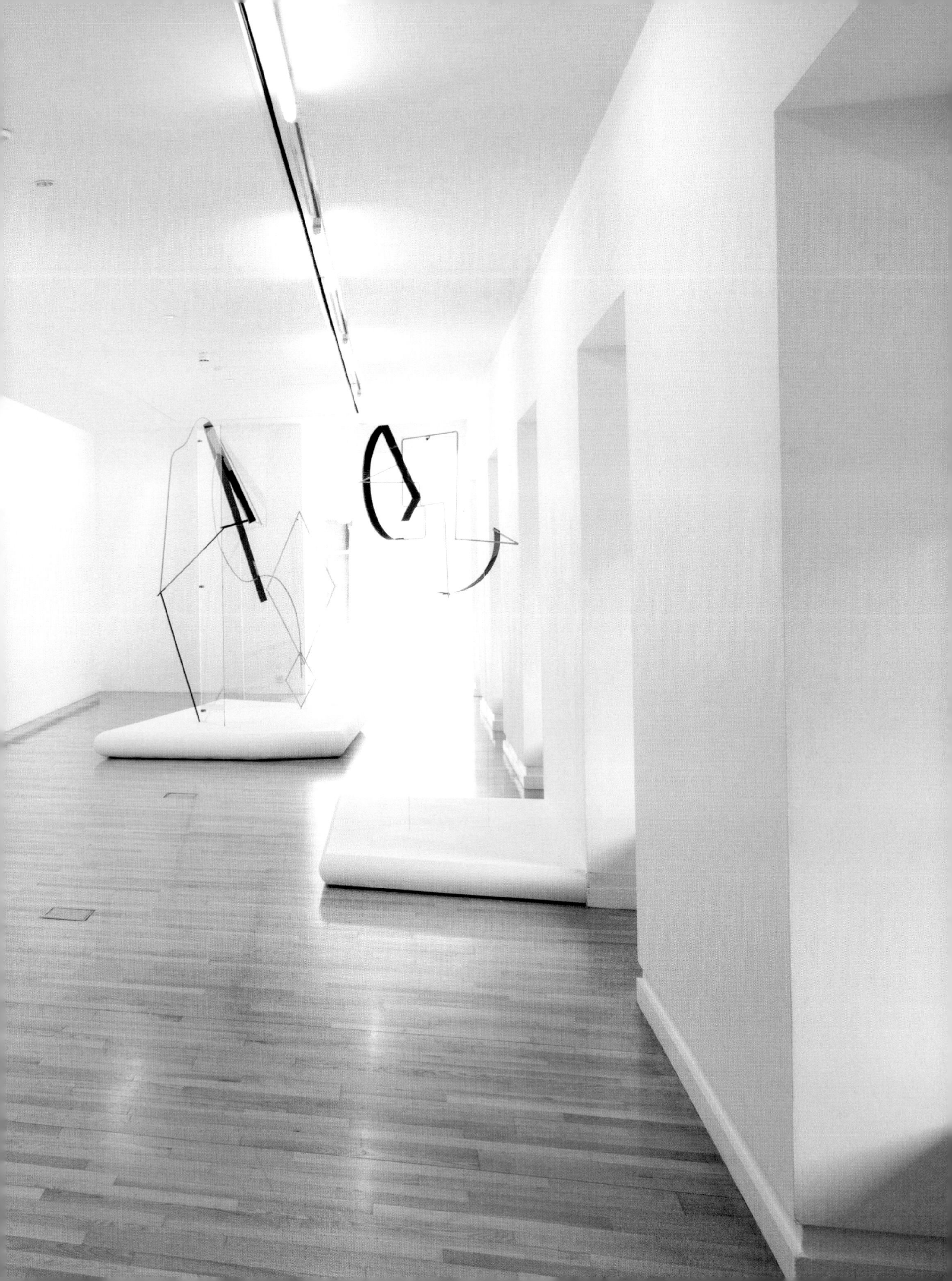

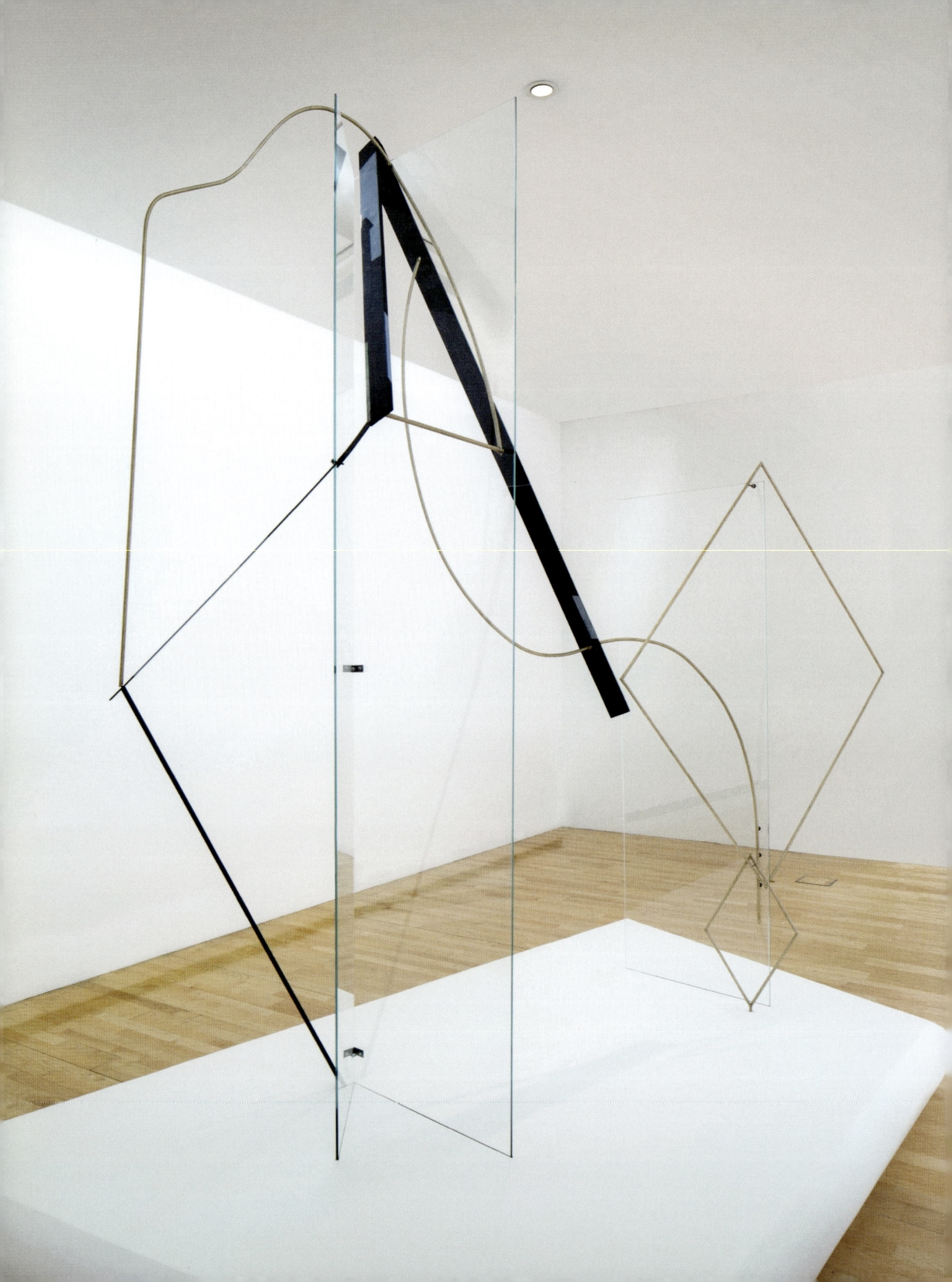

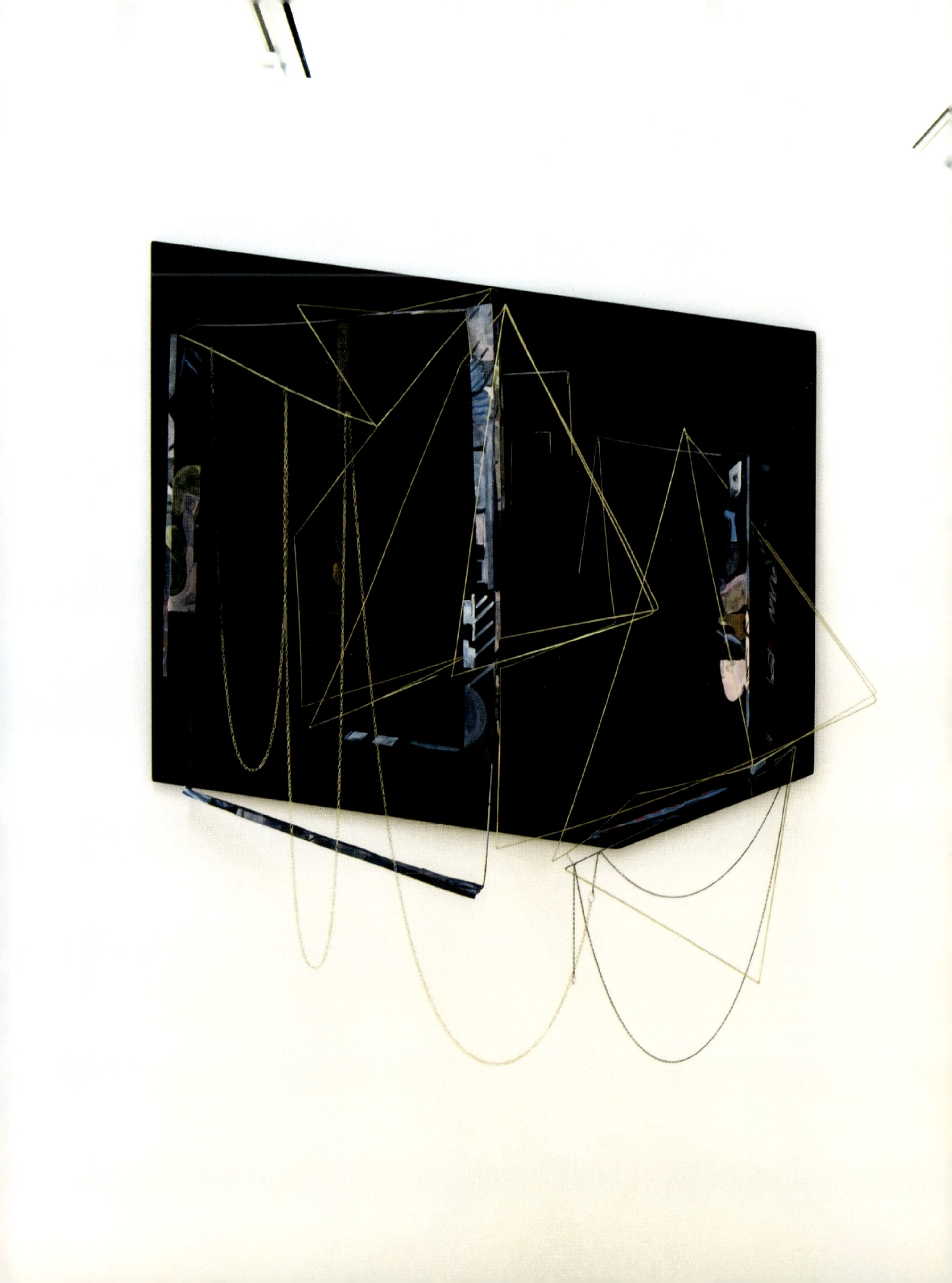

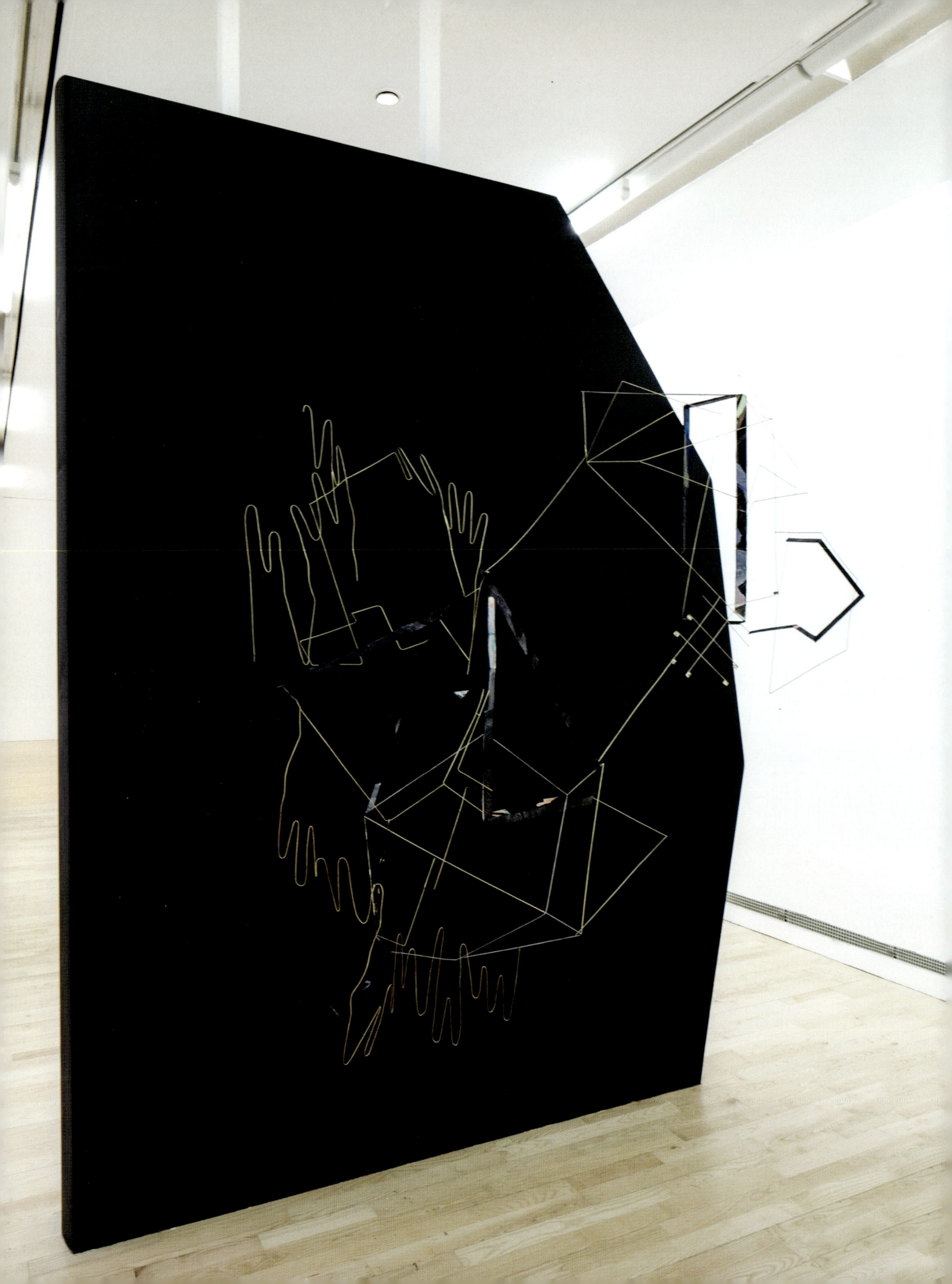

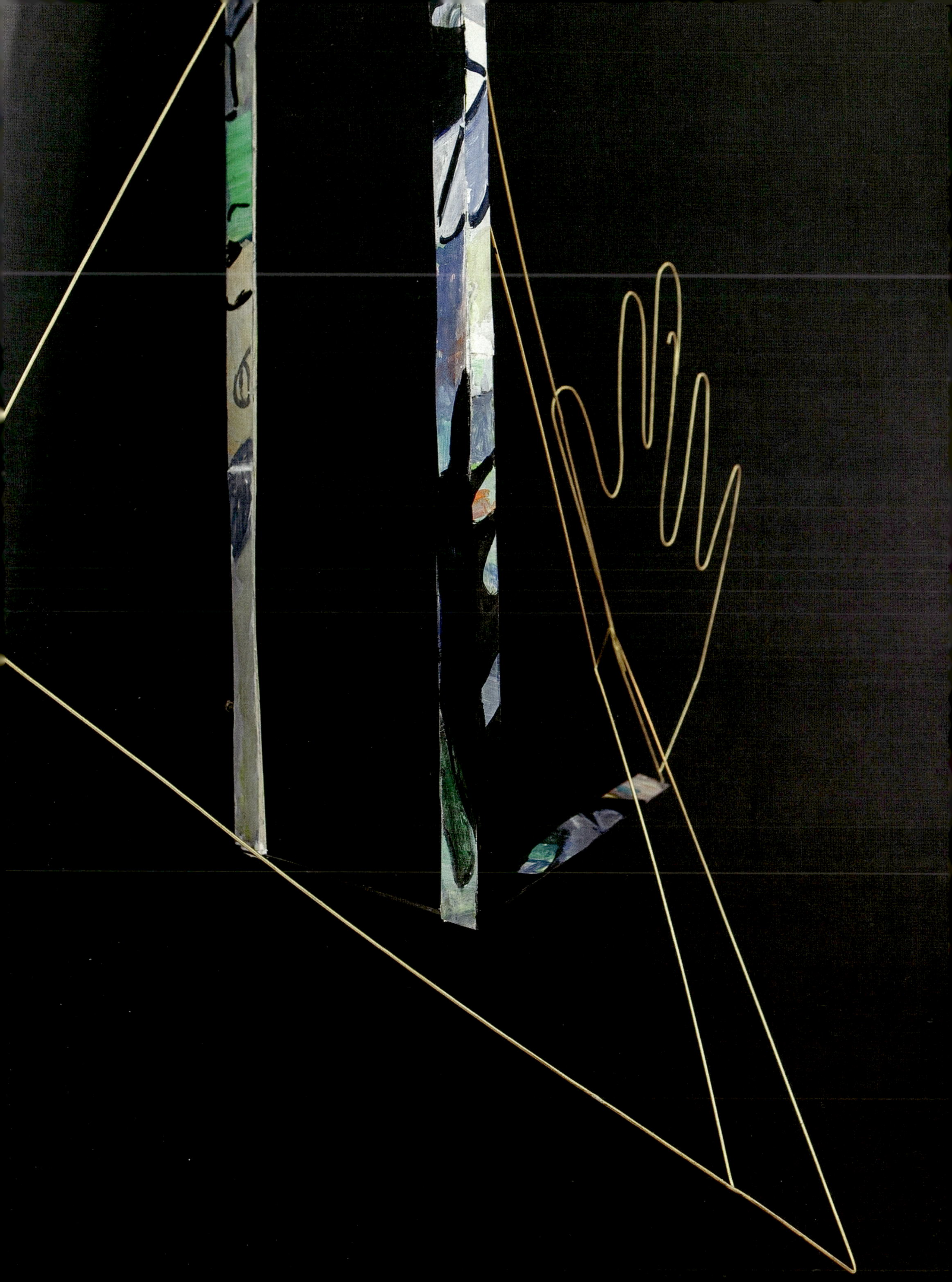

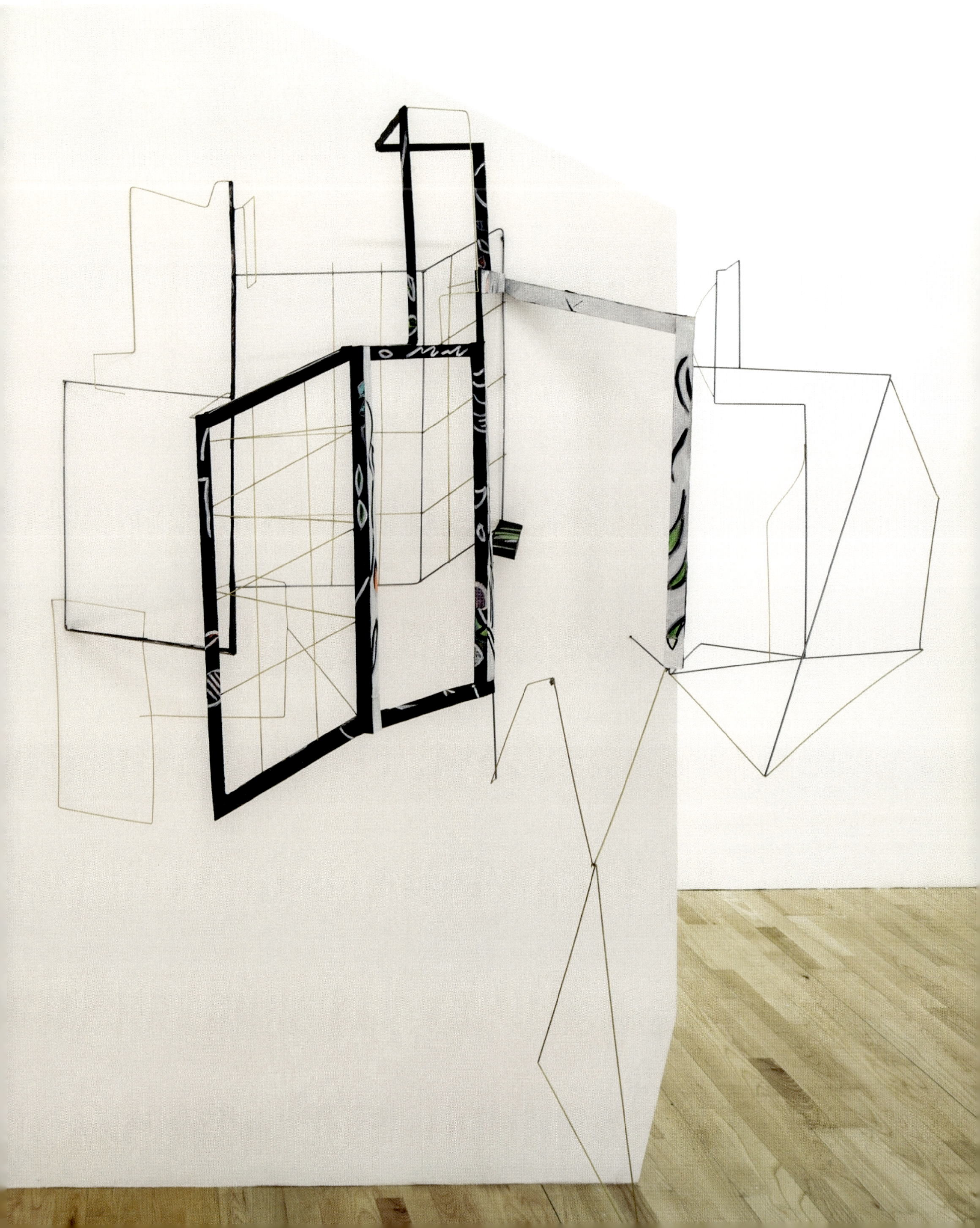

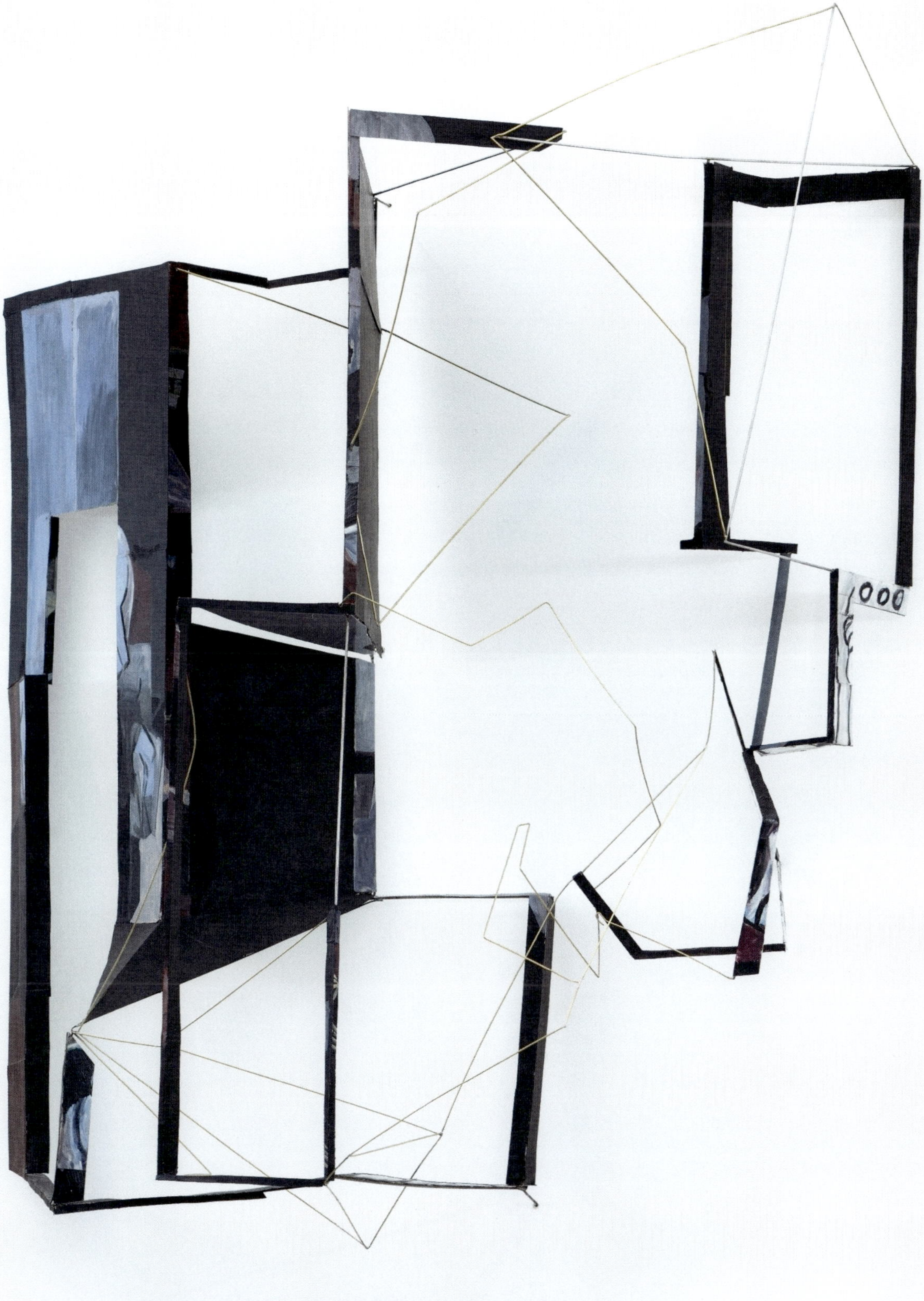

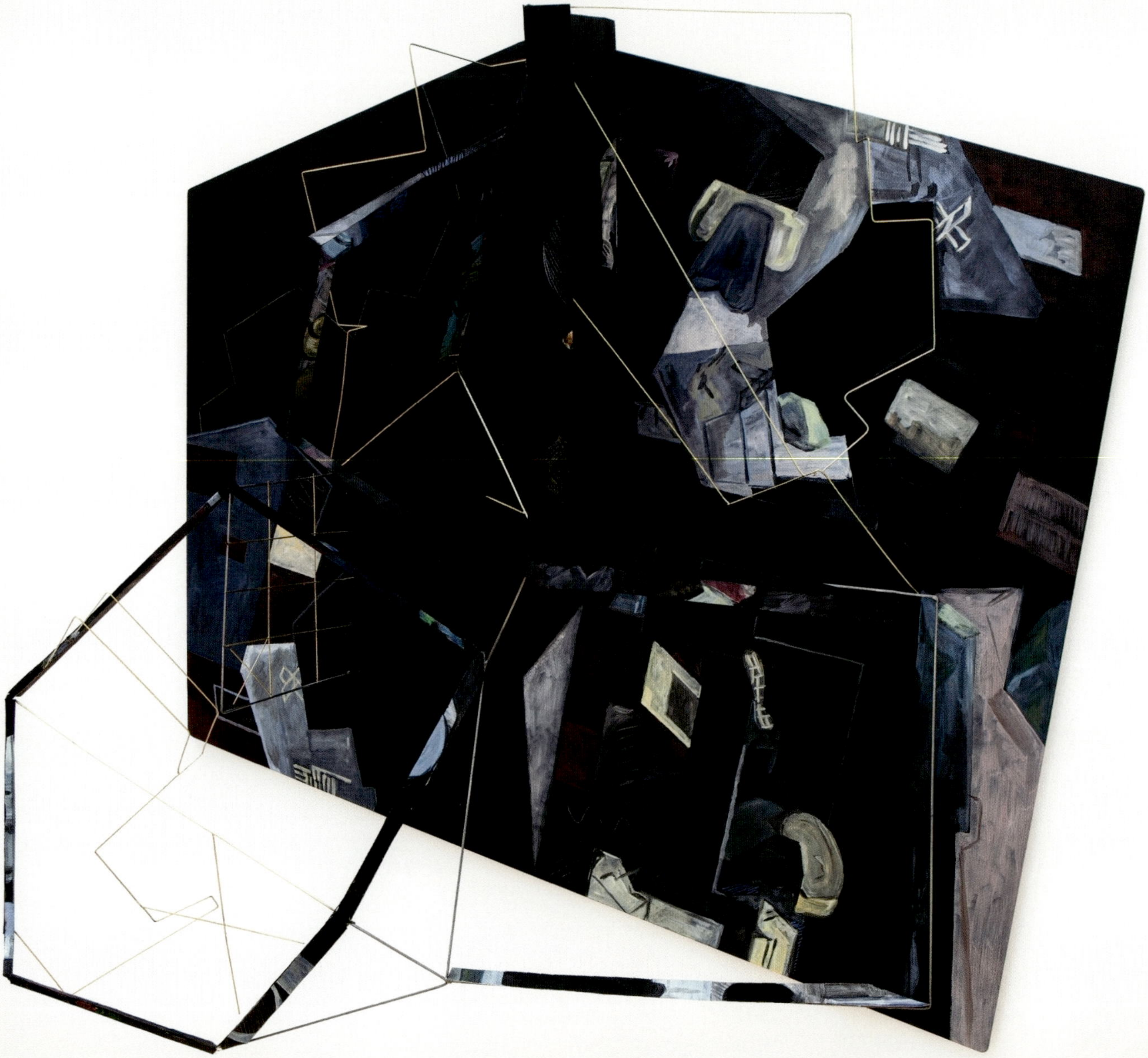

MAKING IT EVEN NEWER

ALI SMITH

Open on Sara Barker's desk face-down when I visit her studio is a copy of a collection of *Imagist Poetry* – a poetic influenced by Cubism and the overt experimentation happening, just over a century ago, in the visual and sculptural arts.

Make it new! this was Ezra Pound's demand, one which still acts like a powerful little magnet at the core of modernist understandings and practices. Pound was, along with H.D., Richard Aldington, F.S. Flint and Amy Lowell, at the centre of the formation of the self-styled Imagiste's aesthetics. 'An "Image",' he wrote, 'is that which presents an intellectual and emotional complex in an instant of time. ... It is the presentation of such a "complex" instantaneously which gives that sense of sudden liberation; that sense of freedom from time limits and space limits; that sense of sudden growth, which we experience in the presence of the greatest works of art.' A single image that produced this complex, in words, Pound said, was worth a lifetime's 'voluminous works'.

Barker is an artist profoundly and consciously influenced by the works of high modernists like Pound, Lowell, Virginia Woolf and Gertrude Stein, especially by the force of structural questioning in the work of the latter two – but also by the sheer lifeforce in a literary questioner of *social* structure like D.H. Lawrence who in his poem 'At the Window' describes how 'pine-trees bend to listen to the autumn wind'; in the poem a scene is made not just cohesive but into a piece of vibrant, vibrating interconnectedness, regardless of divisions and severings, by the act of looking itself – by 'the face that leans from the darkness, intent, with two dark-filled eyes / That watch for ever earnestly from behind the window glass'.

I know Barker is drawn, too, in terms of both the written and the visual-dimensional, to Marcel Duchamp; in an email she sent to me shortly before we met, she included a vivid piece of writing by him, a short paragraph called 'Breeding of Colors'. It begins: '– In the greenhouse – [On a glass plate, color seen transparently]. Mixture of flowers of color i.e. each color still in its optical state', and Barker's work echoes this deliberate, consciously fruitful, seeing process – and the writers and artists to whom she is expressly drawn share something fundamental to this process, and to its outcome: a new transparent framing, via the 'optical state', whose end result is fertility and growth.

When I visited her studio in September 2015 and we sat and talked for a while she told me too about her admiration for Eva Hesse, the 'ingrained knowledge in her work,' and for Cathy Wilkes's work, the 'bringing together of elements' in it and how 'painterly' Wilkes is with her objects, how she makes interrelation, 'beautiful and ugly,' happen, and also for the rawness, the powerful relevance which is never didactic, in her tactile 'spillage'. Barker went on to talk about how, as a student, she herself was drawn to the notion of found objects, spilt things. 'But I decided,' she said, 'that I wanted to make my own stories.' So she began to make sculptural forms out of paper, which she'd work on with graphite 'to change the quality of the material, to make something new'.

Making it new. Yet when I came away from the studio, and although I know all these influences are clearly in play in Barker's work, work which asks us every time to learn to read originally, sculpturally, and in an ever-new way, it was and is something else chiming at the back of the experience of seeing this work, the fleeting ghost of Giacometti, maybe shades of late Matisse or of Matisse's feeling for the textured fabric of things, the tangible or palpable presence of material and simultaneous consideration of the nature of material, yes. But what it really conjured and conjures is a fascinating meld, or maybe weld, of the modern and the classical. It was Victor Pasmore who came unexpectedly to mind, the thought that Barker's work would be completely at home next to Pasmore's, and particularly his *Metamorphosis* works – most especially his linear motifs with this title, and the echo goes further – it goes to Echo, as in Echo and Narcissus – because this work, in some deep-articulated way, conjures Ovid's *Metamorphoses*.

The story of Echo and Narcissus is a story of voice, of reflected or mirrored voice, voice that comes about through a physical distillation and a human transformation into elementals, air and earth, in a story that asks questions about what reflection and repetition make of us. Then there's all the stripping-away and thinning-out, the stripping back to voice at its essence, and back to the original source of music and art, in an Ovidian story like the one when the god Pan has chased and caught a nymph called Syrinx who defies his determination to have her by transforming in his arms into

> a handful of marsh reeds. As he stood, sighing, the wind blew through the reeds, and produced a thin, plaintive sound. The god was enchanted by the new device and by the sweetness of the music. 'You and I shall always talk together so!' he cried. Off he went, the great god Pan, to work out how to fix together, into one single resonant structure, the differing lengths of reed.

The Ovidian conversation is always about formal exchange and renewal. If the modernists were classicists, Ovid is the original modernist, the first maker of things new via the text.

But the moment in the *Metamorphoses* I'm most surprised to find myself thinking of, in relation to Barker's work, is a tiny but shockingly strong detail (and this in itself is akin to the way that a detail of bright rich colour in any close viewing of one of Barker's works will catch the eye out, shock both eye and mind into pleasure) in a story that's framed by, or literally embedded in, a completely different story (again how like Barker's works, which are themselves so often concerned with the consequences and liberations in framing and embedding).

It comes when Ovid tells the story of Arachne, the weaver, a woman gallus enough to challenge the goddess Pallas to a tapestry-making duel. Arachne's tapestries are so shockingly good and beautiful that she actually near defeats the goddess in this duel. But goddesses never lose, and Arachne gets transformed into a spider for her hubris, and at one point in the telling Ovid describes the tapestry that Pallas weaves to demonstrate to this mere groundling exactly what's what, and who has the real power. In one corner of this tapestry the goddess has embroidered a figuring of the legend of *another* goddess annoyed by rivalry, in this case Juno, who's been so piqued by the prettiness of the daughters of a man called Cinyras rivalling her own beauty that she transforms those insolently too-pretty girls into a line of stone steps leading up to the front of a minor temple. (Interestingly, in other versions of this story she also turns their father, who's lying there grieving for his girls with his arms round the stone steps, into a pillar).

When I'd finished my studio visit and come away from Barker's work it was this tiny fragment of story that unexpectedly surfaced; perhaps because of something about its embeddedness, or its repeating echoes, its play of the stony-solid yet still diaphanous, web-like yet tough, or even about the notion of architecture deep in it (Victor Pasmore, I remember, was also an architect). Perhaps it's something about the strength and fragilities of structure-building and myth-making and how much of the human in us goes into the structures we make, buildings or stories. Perhaps it's about control and defiance too, because there's something, though it's almost impossible to articulate, about both these concepts at the core of Barker's work.

Above all, though, it's about the notion of a transformation happening literally, as we watch, via the vehicle – the image, the story, the dimension of the artwork.

Anyway, for now I've just got here, I've just arrived in her studio, down by the Arches in an unexpectedly warm and sunny Glasgow, to talk to her about the upcoming show and the new work she's been doing, and to see some of the new maquette process and new work, and there's no other tense for it but the present tense. This is present tense work, for all its roots in and conduits to the modernist and the classical, and the first thing I can't not notice is that the sunlight and sky light in the place is astonishing, it seems to be playing on several planes all round me like a meditative fairground ride (if there's such a thing), or like I'm at sea or on water, and everything, wherever I glance, is iridescent because so many of the works and the maquettes in the room are reflective so that light shifts round it, them and me at unexpected angles all playing between bluntness and sharpness. I comment on it. Barker tells me about time spent on the Isle of Man, the push of the sea that's become part of her fabric, from her formative years there. She talks about glass and reflection, and about working with glass to modify and make opaqueness, to veil and challenge reflection as well as work with transparency, to change the texture of what we perceive as being just surface. While we're talking a train rattles past the studio so that the sound and the experience of it is actually physical, it shakes the place a little, and by the time the visit's over the regular Helensburgh/Queen Street train and the notion of continuous movement between destinations will have become part of the room and part, too, of the experience of the work, which is all movement between form and form, painting and sculpture, figurative and abstract, metal and air, oil and water, and everything in dialogue, like a natural weighing-up of things is happening in each piece, and even between the pieces as the eye happens on them.

I notice in the most recent work in progress a new level of clear figuration, on the one hand in the shape of human figures and on the other in the inclusion of what look like actual alphabet letters. It is a clearer gesture than I've seen in her work before, towards the conventions of language and of direct figurative shaping. When I ask about it, she tells me she is trying a new move on from the notion (already familiar to those who know her work) of threshold, or simple entrance. She calls it 'a wanting to say more'; I'm intrigued by this because in the past her abstracts have courted but ultimately quite clearly rejected such notions of obvious figuration. It might not survive into the finished work, she tells me; then says, 'but it might, all the same,' and this is the point at which I realize how much her work is about not just this dialogue between its own suggestions and possibilities, but something even more closely and interestingly related to the writing process and language work – the edit.

The language of her work, I realize, is centrally about the space it makes, and the space left (and made) by it, the meaning that's both present and absent. We talk for a bit about the plans for the Fruitmarket show, and how a major feature will be the ways works will either sink into the very walls of the room, actually into the seeming structure of the gallery, or press physically back out into the space of the room, so that the liminalities, and a notion of hidden/revealed perspective dimensions and deceptively fluid architectural structures, in other words a revelation of layers and layerings, will be at the heart of it.

'If you are given no path where the journey is level and easy, / If in your way you find barricade, padlock on door, / Use your inventive wits, come slipping down through a skylight, / Clamber, hand over hand, where a high window swings wide.' This is Ovid again, this time from his *The Art of Love*, here specifically about never being denied, about taking 'the new road of the air' when it looks like you're blocked – like Icarus and Daedalus, with all the resultant risks, and so that your inventiveness will never be defied.

The work in this studio is all a mapping of that new road of the air – it's maybe why Barker uses so much glass, so that her works, in all their dimensionalities, are revelations of the way that air is structure too. So many of the works exist as if suspended in space, hung in pure air. Transparency itself is revealed as structural.

Barker tells me, as we walk round, about her attraction to the colour blue, about the 'security' she senses in 'this fluid colour' and how she is keen to 'enhance the material using the colour of metal, water, light and glass', and I notice that structures that look skeletal and are three-dimensional approach, as if wooing, the two-dimensional, and that her way of working with painting approaches, equally seductively, the three-dimensional, that her structures consciously and wittily defy and surprise you – and are all concerned to reveal that you *can't not see through* them.

It's all about this seeing-through, the seeing through something and the seeing something through: about the transparency of things that seem to refute any such thing. It's about the point at which one thing becomes another, metal becomes painting and vice versa, the point at which structure itself is revealed as strips of colour. Colour acts as a kind of speed, as a kind of casual transformative happening. That shape there looks like a ship's sail, but a sail marked and blotted by sky, as if the whole sky is held in the sail of a ship instead of the other way round.

'I want to make sculpture as provisional as drawing is,' Barker is saying next to me as I notice the burnt metal joints, gold and turquoise, in one maquette, and watch how the morphous and amorphous are in conversation in the works and things-in-progress, as if I'm watching the actual conversation taking place between them. '... the grid-like form which feels more than music,' she is saying next to me, while my eye gets all caught up in the unexpected direction things can and will take, in how straightness will bend – to listen? Like in the Lawrence poem? The maquettes look like figurings of jazz, they look like improvisation made physical, I mean with all the discipline that true improvisation demands. They look like they're playing a tune you know, but that you never expected anyone to be able to bend it quite that way, certainly never expected to find this new and unexpected turn of notes along the line of that so-known tune.

'I wanted to notice something I haven't ever seen,' she says. All round the room the mystery of workaday things – wire, chain, glass, wood – reveals itself, yet leaves the things as they really are. Spray-paint greens and oranges and jagged edges and hooks become a new kind of punctuation, and threshold opens to threshold opening to threshold. The very notion of reflection becomes about structure, about the creation of windows, but windows hung in mid-air, windows unwalled. The train lines outside the studio are mirrored in the maquette surfaces; the inside and outside world are in working harmony in here. There's a sense of both blur and shock at once in the works, and sandblasted marks on the perspex and on the glass reveal the different natures of these materials at the same time as acting as if maths equations have suddenly become 3D biology, as if geometries can be choreographed, or robots can dismantle themselves as you watch so as to reveal to you that they hold paintings at their core, art at heart. The room is like the thought process of a complicated machinery – as if there's nothing that doesn't have a thought process, or maybe a soul, that's able, when released by the right figuring, to rise above it, aura-like, slab-angle colourful. No wonder I balk against the figurative in this new work. Maybe I'm meant to. It asks walls to pierce themselves, it asks structure to strip itself back and be different. The abstract nature of Barker's strips of colour is inarguable, nevertheless they recall and suggest tiny classic oil-painting landscapes. Her celebration of exactness is set beside an equal celebration of approximation.

Over on the far wall there's a corkboard covered in pliers, hammers, saws, spanners, grippers, hanging on nails. Where the occasional tool has been taken off the wall, the pencil outline which shows what tool should be hanging there is still there, like proof of its absence/presence in one. I look at a pair of pliers, next to a pair of pliers that isn't there, the pencil outline for the gone object, and Barker, standing next to me, tells me about her interest in the premise at the heart of anything sculptural, very simple, very complex – simply/complexly about making things stand up.

She tells me she began as a painter, and how first, more and more drawn to the relationship between the dimensions, she painted on aluminium, 'then cut it up,' she says. The impetus, she explains, is that dimension, demands your interaction with it. Plus, she says, it was like a liberation from the working process, to paint something them cut it up – especially after you've worked and worked on it.

'With the cutters, it's like you can draw again. It's construction and deconstruction simultaneously.' Then she tells me about the importance in her work of welding and how, having cut up a painting, she will work to make 'line and surface come together.' When she first began this practice, she says, the metal started as props to hold the painting out and up, then the metal became playful geometrically, mattered on its own terms, started to fall off, or maybe out of, the wall, 'and I found myself asking: what would it be like to be able to walk through something two dimensional?'

Does her work want to separate or connect its viewers from it or with it? I ask myself, and the answer, of course, is both. There's glass and of course you can see through it, so she sandblasts it, covers it with lines and blurs and star-breaks, to reveal its texture and give it its own language, as if to make glass itself legible, to allow us to get to grips with it, anew, as the material it is. The very notion of welding is about the pressure put on things by energy – heat or electricity – to make one thing out of more than one thing. *To join closely*, that's what to weld means. Its older obsolete meanings include *to melt*, and also a little flowering plant, and also a variant of the verb *to wield*.

In this way, the whole room flowers, wields force and energy and by this is becoming something else, becoming about edits and connections, becoming volatile. The sculpture acts to make you engage with the spatial. Sculpture, Barker says, is a gift of a block of time. 'Sculpture is about freezing time.'

I came away from the studio. On the one hand, there was this expressed notion, the freezing of time; on the other, I was thinking of Pasmore, the so-modern open play of possibilities. Then I remembered this:

> deny me life and death by changing me into some other form.
> Ovid's *Metamorphoses*.

The work, even in maquette form, in its sublime improvisational process, feels pre-ordained. Hope is somehow deep in the process, and the process is about energy, limitation, freedom from parameters – and also the artist's relationship with those parameters.

'Ever-inventive nature continually produces one shape from another. Nothing in the entire universe ever perishes, believe me, but things vary, and adopt new form.' *Metamorphoses*, again. Metamorphosis, again and again, is Sara Barker's nature.

C.V. on land and in sea
brass and stainless steel rod,
sand-blasted perspex, folded
aluminium sheet, automotive paint

drawing, holding, wearing, weaving
is complicated
brass and steel rod

Opened this page at a discordant
woman in a veil in bits
brass and steel rod

Sea heaves in a glass
brass rod, folded aluminium sheet,
perspex, automotive paint

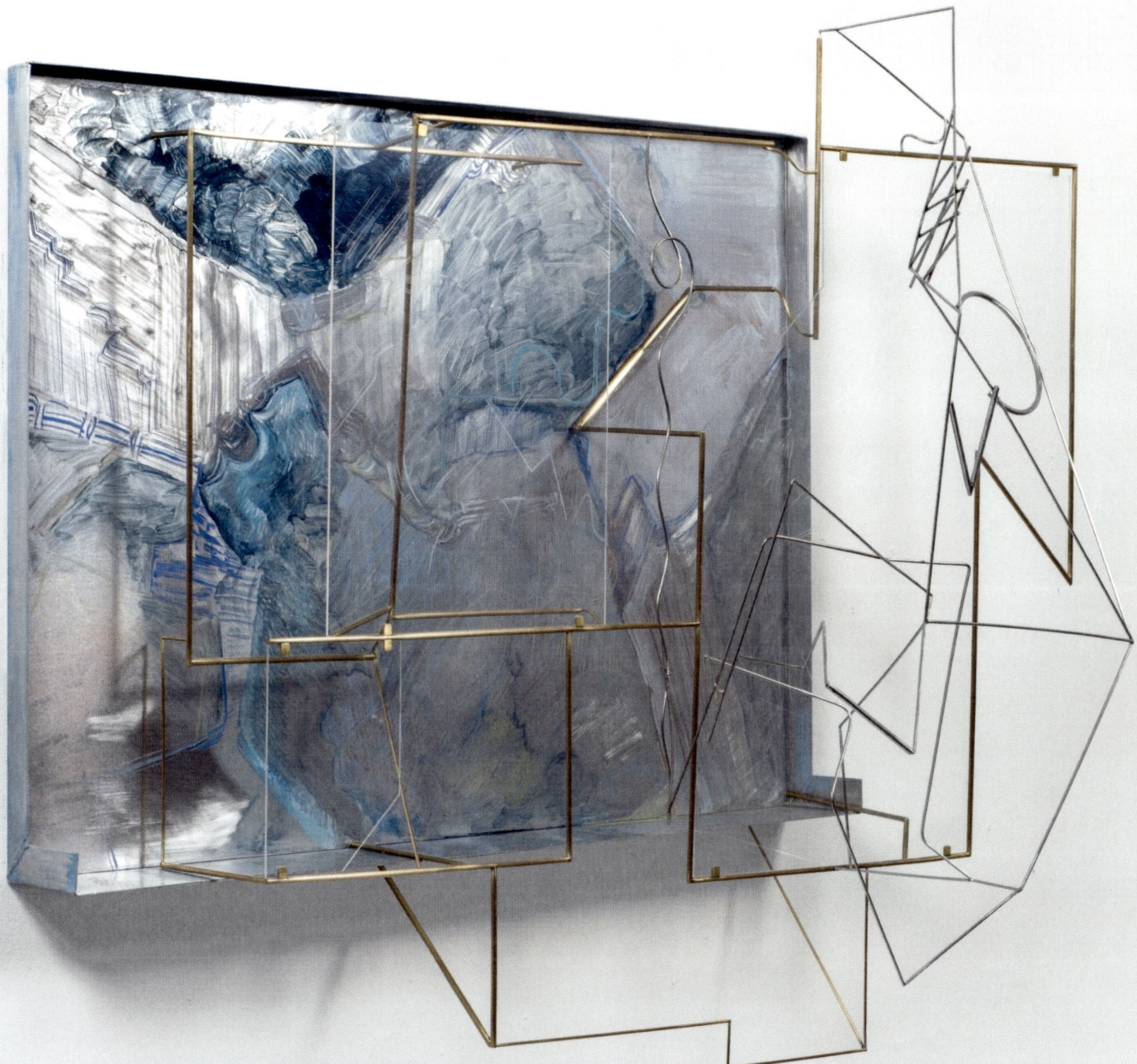

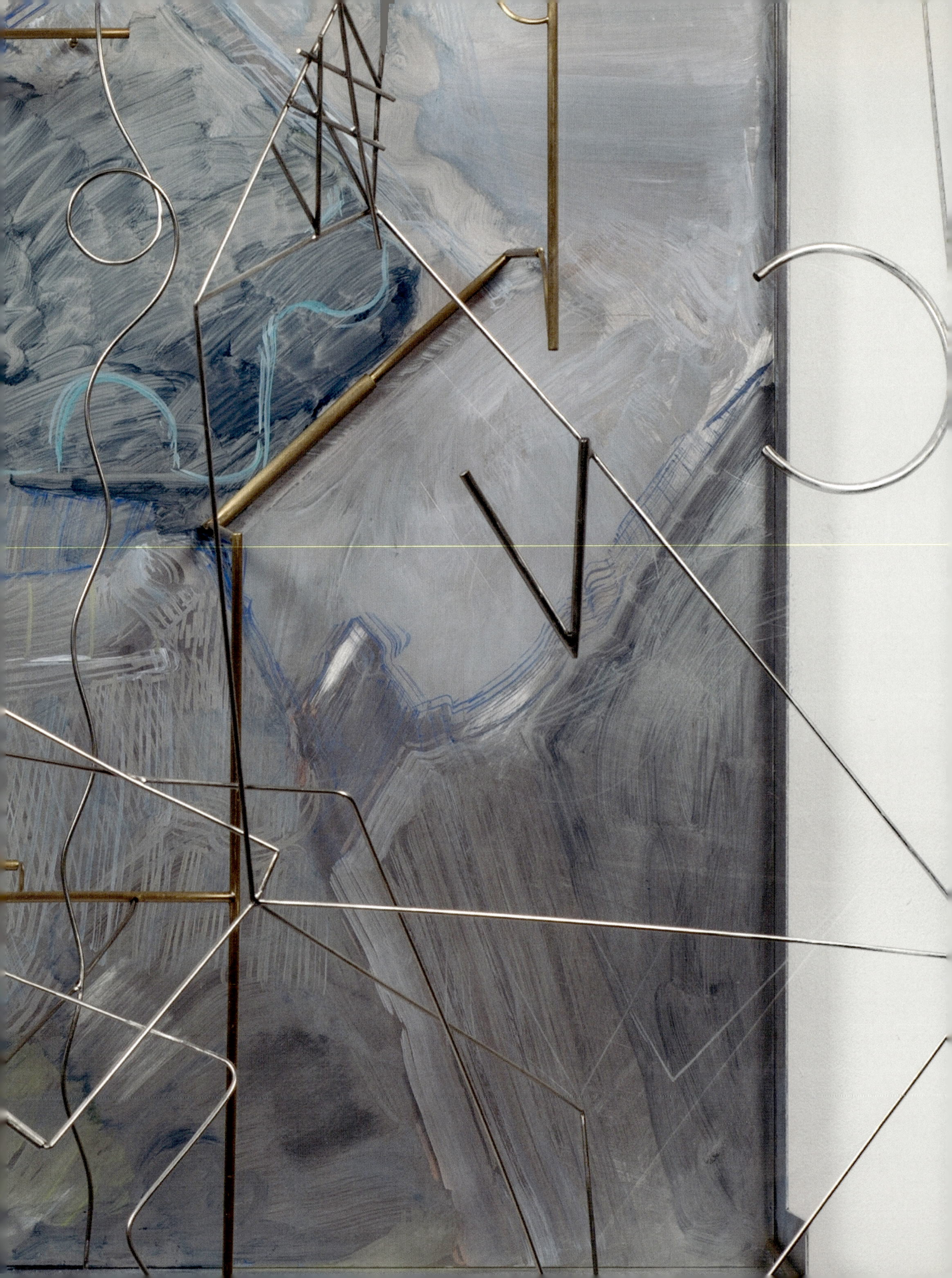

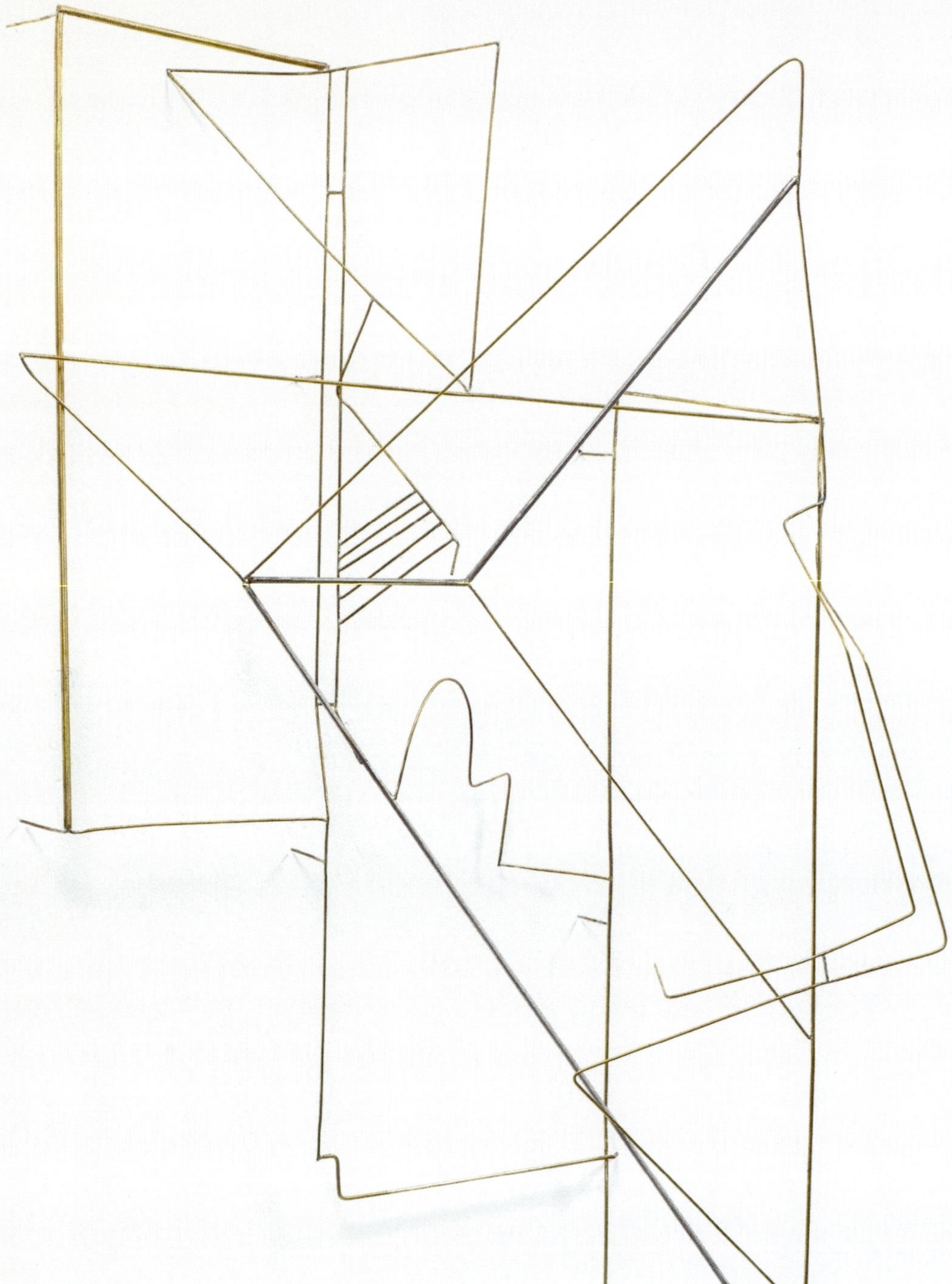

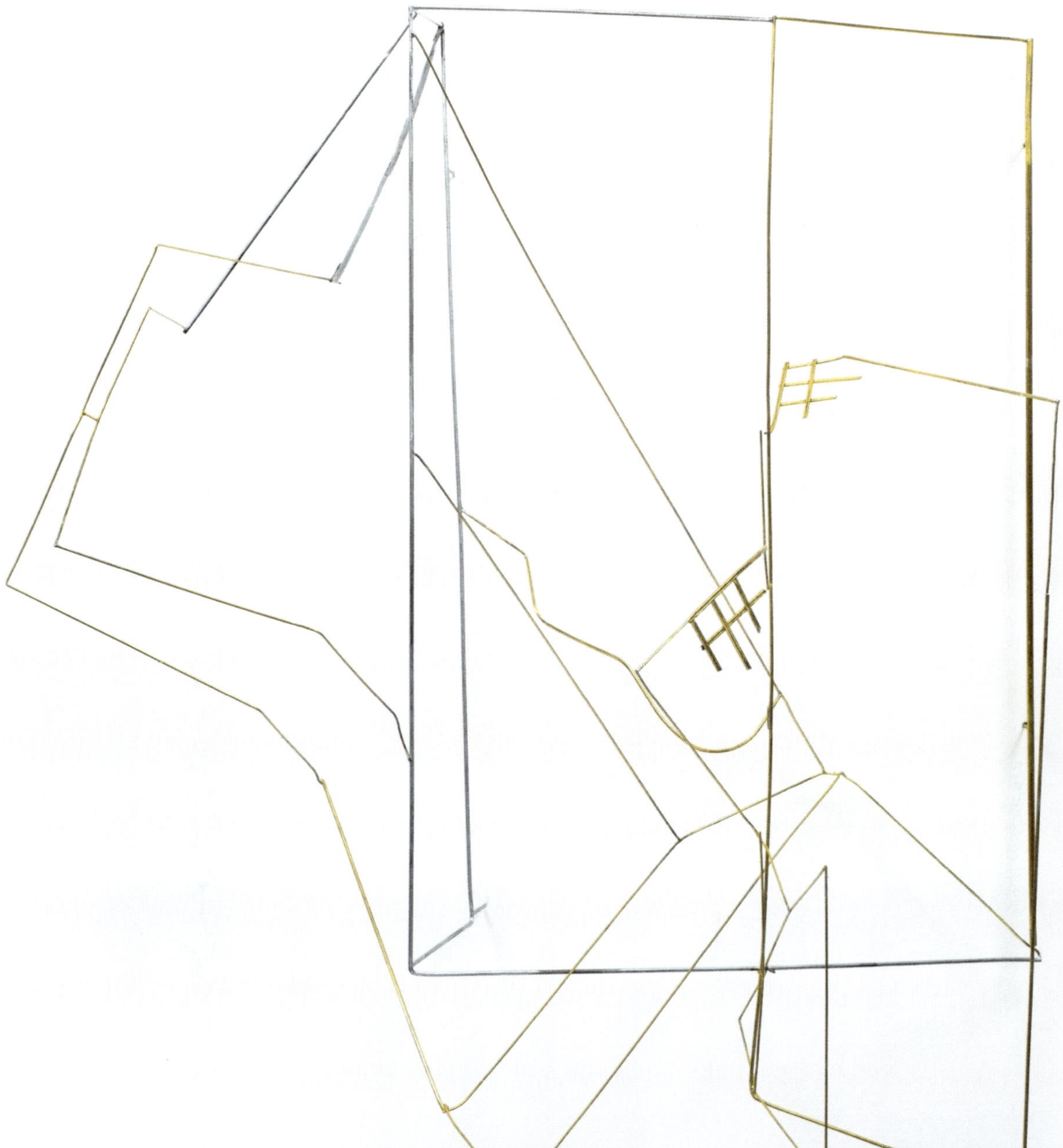

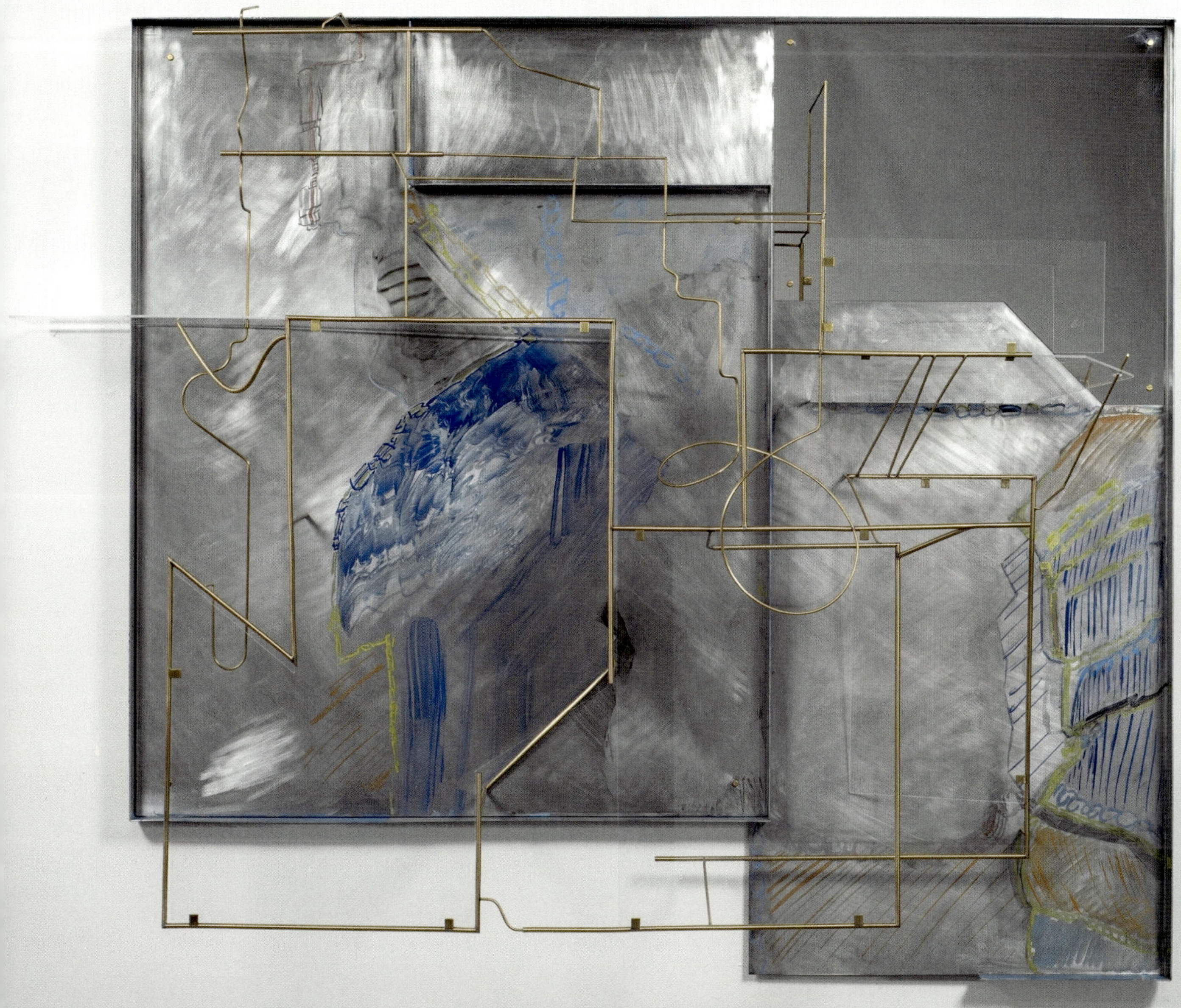

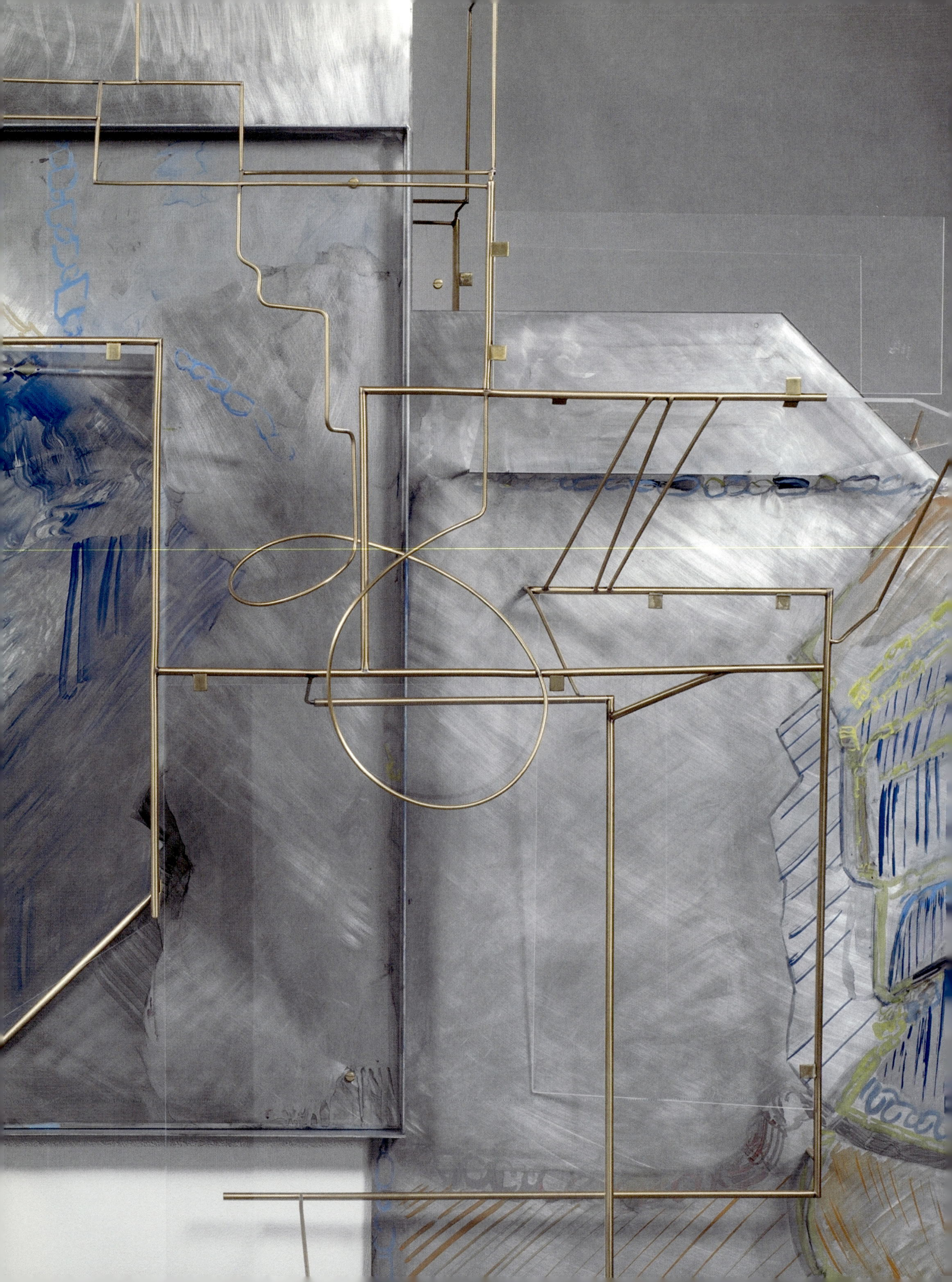

LIST OF ILLUSTRATIONS

9, 10 (detail)
geographies of Dust and Air
moving parts out of night, 2015
Brass and stainless steel rod, folded aluminium sheet, glass, perspex, automotive paint, spray paint
158 x 123.5 x 104 cm
Courtesy the artist; Mary Mary, Glasgow; carlier | gebauer, Berlin; The Approach, London

13,14 (detail)
Minerva made a dream to order Patterns she saw as signs, 2015
Stainless steel and brass rod, folded aluminium sheet, glass, perspex, automotive paint, spray paint
175 x 120 x 69 cm
Courtesy the artist; Mary Mary, Glasgow; carlier | gebauer, Berlin; The Approach, London

17, 18 (detail)
What's the medium?
A medium for their mediums
CHANGE-THE-SETTING, 2015
Stainless steel rod, folded aluminium sheet, glass, perspex, automotive paint, spray paint
142.5 x 107 x 26.5 cm
Courtesy the artist; Mary Mary, Glasgow; carlier | gebauer, Berlin, The Approach, London

23
The Blue Woman, 2008
Cardboard, concrete, acrylic paint, wooden table-plinth
87 x 70 x 70 cm; plinth: 120 x 103 x 72 cm
Collection Martin Z. Margulies, Miami

24 (detail), 25
High Windows, 2008
Concrete, paint, cardboard, wooden table, wood filler
82 x 145 x 36 cm; plinth: 100 x 130 x 70 cm
Collection Martin Z. Margulies, Miami

27
abject posture, 2008
Clay, cement, cardboard, paint, mahogany
102 x 78 x 69 cm
Collection Martin Z. Margulies, Miami

28
unfolding arms behind my back, 2009
Cardboard, cement, clay, woodfiller, acrylic paint, plywood, mahogany
118 x 220 x 79 cm
Courtesy carlier | gebauer, Berlin

31
index finger traces the outline, 2011
Steel, aluminium, oil paint, gouache,
grey filler, bolts
220 x 105 x 40 cm
Louisiana Museum of Modern Art.
Acquired with funding from Museumsfonden

32
Salone, 2008
Cardboard, cement, plywood, acrylic paint
110 x 98 x 1 cm
Collection of Gregory R. Miller and Michael Wiener,
New York

37
her point of view, 2011
Steel, aluminium, various paints, fillers, rivets
227 x 77 x 39 cm
Private Collection, Copenhagen

39
Fenestra, 2010
Aluminium, gouache paint, water-based
primer, polyester resin, glue on painted
steel and glass table
102 x 135 x 10 cm; table: 58 x 163 x 80 cm
The Saatchi Gallery, London

40
La Leçon de piano, 2010
Aluminium sheet, oil-based primer, oil paint,
polyester resin on glass and steel table
119 x 74 x 19 cm; table: 83 x 89 x 46 cm
The Saatchi Gallery, London

42, 43 (detail)
washable colour, 2012
Stainless steel round bar, aluminium sheet,
watercolour, pencil crayon
210 x 91 x 30 cm
Courtesy Mary Mary, Glasgow

45
story of a house, 2012
Stainless steel round bar, aluminium sheet,
various paints
119 x 73 x 15 cm
Collection of Bill and Sue Kidd, Toronto

47
Watercolour seen, 2010
Steel, aluminium, primer, cardboard, grey metal filler,
watercolour, glue, rivets, bolts
200 x 105 x 50 cm
Collection of Gregory R. Miller and Michael Wiener,
New York

49
representing a sketch, 2012
Aluminium sheet, stainless steel round bar,
various paints
220 x 80 x 23 cm
No Bad Collection, Fife

50
Woman at a Window, 2012
Aluminium sheet, brass rod, steel rod, balsa wood,
acrylic paint, gouache, metal filler
214 x 57 x 64 cm
David Roberts Collection, London

52
conversions, 2011
Steel, aluminium, various paints
215 x 115 x 65 cm
The Saatchi Gallery, London

65
flowering of the rod, 2011
Aluminium, steel, gouache, water-based
oil paint, chain
210 x 106 x 120 cm
Courtesy carlier | gebauer, Berlin

66, 67 (detail)
Aquaria, 2012
Aluminium sheet, steel, canvas, watercolour,
oil paint, pastel, filler, rivets
222 x 77 x 62 cm
Sammlung Goetz, Munich

68
walls and clouds backing the view, 2012
Steel and brass rod, aluminium sheet, oil paint,
aluminium paint, metal filler
97 x 62 x 44 cm
No Bad Collection, Fife

71
Draft overlapped, 2012
Steel rod, brass rod, aluminium sheet, oil paint,
canvas, metal filler, glass
102 x 62 x 46 cm
David Roberts Collection, London

72
Universal arrangement and Staging, 2012
Steel rod, steel flat bar, aluminium sheet, gouache, acrylic paint, metal filler, mirror and steel base
233 x 90 x 122 cm
Courtesy Mary Mary, Glasgow

75
Love letter, 2012
Aluminium sheet, steel rod, steel bar, canvas, oil paint, watercolour, acrylic paint, aquarelle, metal filler on steel and mirror plinth
216 x 119 x 86 cm
The Saatchi Gallery, London

77
Adolescent, 2012
Steel rod, brass rod, aluminium sheet, canvas, oil paint, acrylic paint, metal filler
130 x 90 x 84 cm
Sheldon Inwentash and Lynn Factor, Toronto

78
Seascape proposal, 2012
Steel rod, aluminium sheet, acrylic paint, gouache, metal filler
96 x 59 x 72 cm
Courtesy carlier | gebauer, Berlin

83
Composition with furling symphonia, 2013
Brass and steel rod, aluminium sheet, gold powder, aluminium powder, watercolour, gouache, metal primer, filler
108 x 72 x 40 cm
S and A Abu Ghazaleh Collection

84, 85 (detail)
sampler, 2013
Steel and brass rod, aluminium sheet, various paints, filler
145 x 59 x 70 cm
Collection of Robert and Nicky Wilson

87
Satellite, 2013
Brass and steel rod, canvas, aluminium, various paints and fillers
165 x 114 x 62 cm
No Bad Collection, Fife

88
Matters, 2013
Plywood, aluminium, various paints, filler, brass rod
122 x 116 x 55 cm
Private Collection

91 (detail), 92
trawling (with triangles) – pin, 2013
Brass and steel rod, aluminium sheet, various paints, filler, blackboard paint
123 x 87 x 34 cm
Courtesy Mary Mary, Glasgow

97, 98, 99 (details)
Sara Barker and Ryder Architecture
The subtle knife, 2013
Brass, copper, aluminium, steel components and fixings, plywood, cement, various paints, glass
695 x 810 x 416 cm
Commissioned by BALTIC Centre for Contemporary Art, Gateshead

101, 102 (detail), 104 (detail)
Patterns, 2013
Glass, painted aluminium, brass, foundation of marble chipped whitecrete, steel fixings
369 x 344 x 294 cm
Courtesy Mary Mary, Glasgow

107, 108 (detail)
Separation in the Evening (a celestial blossom before the yellow house), 2015
Stainless steel, stainless steel rod, brass rod, paint
450 x 400 x 240 cm
Collection of Robert and Nicky Wilson

110 (detail), 111, 112 (detail)
Projections of a family held in space, 2015
Brass rod, mirror polished stainless steel panels, painted aluminium panels, painted aluminium plinth, bespoke stainless steel fixings and brackets
400 x 485 x 385 cm
Private Collection, Frankfurt

117
Outcast Letter, 2014
Toughened glass, brass rod, aluminium section, blackboard paint, oil paint
209 x 50 x 74 cm; plinth: 20 x 60 x 60 cm
Courtesy Mary Mary, Glasgow

118–19
Cross-sectioned feelings, 2014
Toughened glass, brass and steel rod, steel flat bar, aluminium, blackboard paint, oil paint
272 x 78 x 60 cm; plinth: 21 x 178 x 140 cm
Courtesy carlier | gebauer, Berlin

120
In semi-darkness she reclines and pretends to read..., 2014
Toughened glass, brass rod, steel flat bar, aluminium section, blackboard paint, oil paint
254 x 277 x 90 cm; plinth: 20 x 145 x 177 cm
Courtesy Mary Mary, Glasgow

123
loopholes of self expression, 2014
Aluminium sheet, brass and steel rod, steel, oil paint, blackboard paint, chalk
145 x 145 x 39 cm
Private Collection, Glasgow

124, 125 (detail)
HOURS BECOME HANDS (Foliage of Palms), 2014
Aluminium sheet, brass and steel rod, various paints, brass fixings
175 x 210 x 42 cm
Courtesy carlier | gebauer, Berlin

127
The Human Family, 2014
Aluminium sheet, brass and steel rod, various paints, brass fixings
162 x 172 x 55 cm
Private Collection, Zürich

129
cut up dream and fold in time/order/space, 2014
Aluminium sheet, brass and steel rod, oil paint, blackboard paint, chalk
157 x 132 x 72 cm
Courtesy Mary Mary, Glasgow

130
Vase painting from a cylix: discussing a picture, 2014
Aluminium sheet, brass and steel rod, oil paint, blackboard paint, steel, chalk
140 x 142 x 47 cm
Collection Selbart Association

141, 142 (detail)
C.V. on land and in sea, 2015
Brass and stainless steel rod, sand-blasted perspex, folded aluminium sheet, automotive paint
108 x 128 x 61 cm
Collection Sema Gulez

144
drawing, holding, wearing, weaving is complicated, 2015
Brass and steel rod
83 x 50 x 39 cm
Courtesy Mary Mary, Glasgow

145
Opened this page at a discordant woman in a veil in bits, 2015
Brass and steel rod
78 x 74 x 39 cm
Private Collection, Wiltshire

147, 148 (detail)
Sea heaves in a glass, 2015
Brass rod, folded aluminium sheet, perspex, automotive paint
114.5 x 139 x 22 cm
The Whitworth, The University of Manchester

LENDERS TO THE EXHIBITIONS

Collection of Gregory R. Miller and Michael Wiener, New York
David Roberts Collection, London
The Saatchi Gallery, London
Collection of Robert and Nicky Wilson

PHOTOGRAPHERS' CREDITS

Bernd Borchardt
Ruth Clark
Colin Davison
Alan Dimmick
Robert Chase Heishman
Keith Hunter, courtesy Jupiter Artland
Alan Macateer, courtesy Glasgow Museums
Stephen Robinson
Lewis Ronald
Max Slaven
Jan Søndergaard
Todd White Art Photography

SARA BARKER

BORN 1980, MANCHESTER
LIVES AND WORKS IN GLASGOW

EDUCATION

1999–2003 BA (Hons) Fine Art, Painting, Glasgow School of Art
1998–1999 History of Art, University of Glasgow

SOLO EXHIBITIONS

2016
Ikon Gallery, Birmingham
The Fruitmarket Gallery, Edinburgh

2015
Outdoor work commission, CASS Sculpture Foundation, Goodwood, West Sussex
Permanent sculptural commission, Jupiter Artland, Edinburgh

2014
for myself and strangers, Gallery of Modern Art, Glasgow
I become almost a shadow, carlier | gebauer, Berlin

2013
The subtle knife, with Ryder Architecture, BALTIC Centre for Contemporary Art, Gateshead
THE THINGS THAT ARE SOLID, ABSORBED AND STILL, Mary Mary, Glasgow
Patterns, Jupiter Artland, Edinburgh Art Festival commission

2012
Mary Mary at 45 Alexandra Park Street, Glasgow
Woman at a Window, Stuart Shave/Modern Art, London

2010
Images, Mary Mary, Glasgow

2009
FOUR, Dublin

2008
Present Future, Artissima Art Fair, Turin
hanging a way of dressing, Glasgow Project Room

2007
Mary Mary, Glasgow

2006
New Work Scotland, Collective Gallery, Edinburgh

SELECTED GROUP EXHIBITIONS

2016
Geographies of Dust and Air: Leonor Antunes, Sara Barker, Germaine Kruip, Manuela Leinhoß, Bojan Šarcević, Mary Mary, Glasgow

2015
Signal Failure, Pace, London

2013
The End of the 20th Century: The Best Is Yet to Come, Nationalgalerie im Hamburger Bahnhof – Museum für Gegenwart, Berlin
Sara Barker and Barbara Kasten, Mary Mary at 10 Northington Street, London
The Gravity of Things, Galeria Quadrado Azul, Lisbon
Laura Aldridge, Sara Barker and Sue Tompkins, Shane Campbell Gallery, Chicago
New Order: British Art Today, The Saatchi Gallery, London
Drawing : Sculpture, The Drawing Room, London
The Geometry of Things: Markus Amm, Sara Barker, Charlotte Moth and Robin Watkins, GAK, Bremen
Least common denominator, M.1 / Arthur Boskamp-Stiftung, Hohenlockstedt

2012
A House of Leaves. Second Movement, David Roberts Art Foundation, London
Tracing the Century: Drawing from Tate Collection, Tate Liverpool
Drawing : Sculpture, Leeds Art Gallery
Pink Caviar: Recent Acquisitions, Louisiana Museum of Modern Art, Humlebæk
Studio 58: Women Artists in Glasgow Since WWII, Mackintosh Museum, Glasgow School of Art

2011
Frauenzimmer – Sara Barker, Karla Black, Carol Bove, Thea Djordjadze, Isa Genzken, Kitty Kraus, Tatiana Trouvé, Museum Morsbroich, Leverkusen
Look with all your eyes, look, Frith Street Gallery, London
Sediments. Sara Barker and Lars Tygesen, Christian Andersen, Copenhagen

2010
Somiglianze non sensibili: Sara Barker, Bettina Buck, Chiara Camoni, Nicolas Chardon, Maria Loboda, Marie Lund, Gyan Panchal, Galerie Opdahl, Stavanger and Galerie Opdahl, Berlin
Sara Barker / Jessica Rankin, carlier | gebauer, Berlin
Zero Budget Biennial, Paris

2009
The Morning After the Big Fire: Sara Barker and Michael Samuels, Villa du Parc Contemporary Art Center, Annemasse
Taj Mahal Travellers, Galerie Nordenhake, Stockholm
La Importancia del Pez Cebra, Pilar Parra and Romero, Madrid
The Actuality of the Idea, Stuart Shave/Modern Art, London

2008
Base:Object, Andrea Rosen Gallery, New York
Open Eye Club, Tramway, Glasgow
Claire Barclay, Sara Barker, Neil Clements, Sally Osborn, Jonathan Owen, Albrecht Schäfer, doggerfisher, Edinburgh

2007
SV07: Members' Show, Studio Voltaire, London

2006
Peaton House, Cove Park, Argyll and Bute
Magazine 06, Edinburgh Sculpture Workshop
Mantua Art Festival, Roscommon
Transmission Members show, Glasgow

2005
Re-Escape, Hamburg
Untitled, Transmission, Glasgow

2004
Best in Show: The Embassy Members' Show, Embassy Gallery, Edinburgh
Shadow Lives, Emerge Gallery, Glasgow
Sara Barker and Lotte Gertz, Mary Mary Project Space, Glasgow

ACKNOWLEDGEMENTS

This book is published on the occasion of the exhibition

SARA BARKER: CHANGE-THE-SETTING
12 March – 5 June 2016
The Fruitmarket Gallery, Edinburgh

24 September – 27 November 2016
Ikon Gallery, Birmingham

EXHIBITION SUPPORTED BY
The Henry Moore Foundation

PUBLISHED BY
The Fruitmarket Gallery
45 Market Street, Edinburgh, EH1 1DF
Tel: +44 (0) 131 225 2383
fruitmarket.co.uk

and

Ikon Gallery
1 Oozells Square, Brindleyplace
Birmingham, B1 2HS
Tel: +44 (0) 121 248 0708
ikon-gallery.org

Edited by Fiona Bradley and Jonathan Watkins
Designed and typeset by Elizabeth McLean
Assisted by Susan Gladwin and Roma Piotrowska

PUBLICATION SUPPORTED BY
Mary Mary
Suite 2/1, 6 Dixon Street, Glasgow, G1 4AX
Tel: +44 (0) 141 226 2257
marymarygallery.co.uk

carlier | gebauer
Markgrafenstraße 67, D-10969 Berlin
Tel: +49 (0)30 2400 863-0
carliergebauer.com

The Approach
1st Floor, 47 Approach Road
Bethnal Green, London E2 9LY
Tel: +44 (0) 20 8983 3878
theapproach.co.uk

ISBN 978-1-908612-38-0

SARA BARKER THANKS
Tim and Sebastian Facey, Fiona Bradley and the team at The Fruitmarket Gallery and Jonathan Watkins and the team at Ikon Gallery, Ruth Clark, Simon Hopkins, Graeme Raeburn, Will Jamieson and all at Scott Associates, Mary Mary, Glasgow, carlier | gebauer, Berlin and The Approach, London. And gratefully acknowledges the support of the Open Project Fund from Creative Scotland.

The Henry Moore
Foundation

THE FRUITMARKET GALLERY is a company limited by guarantee, registered in Scotland No. 87888 and registered as a Scottish Charity No. SC 005576.

VAT No. 398 2504 21.

Registered Office: 45 Market Street,
Edinburgh, EH1 1DF

The Fruitmarket Gallery shows the work of some of the world's most important Scottish and international artists, helping people engage with it in the way that is best for them – for free. We are committed to making contemporary art accessible without compromising art or underestimating audiences.

The Fruitmarket Gallery is not-for-profit and exhibitions are always free. Our work is supported through Regular Funding from Creative Scotland, income from the café and bookshop as well as fundraising from trusts, foundations, donations and sponsorship. Please support us to stay independent, ambitious and free.

Publishing is an intrinsic part of The Fruitmarket Gallery's creative programme. Books are conceived as part of the exhibition-making process, extending the reach and life of each exhibition and offering artists and curators a second space to present their work.

CREATIVE SCOTLAND
ALBA | CHRUTHACHAIL

IKON Gallery Limited trading as Ikon
Registered charity no: 528892

VAT No. 112 3268 13.

Registered Address: 1 Oozells Square,
Birmingham, B1 2HS

Ikon is an internationally acclaimed contemporary art gallery situated in central Birmingham. Housed in a magnificent neo-gothic school building, it is an educational charity and works to encourage public engagement with contemporary art through exhibiting new work in a context of debate and participation. It offers free entry to all.

Ikon receives revenue funding from Arts Council England and Birmingham City Council, grants from trusts and foundations, as well as donations and sponsorship. We welcome new supporters.

IKON Birmingham City Council Supported using public funding by ARTS COUNCIL ENGLAND